Is It Time to Reform Social Security?

EDWARD M. GRAMLICH

Is It Time to Reform Social Security?

Ann Arbor
The University of Michigan Press

First paperback edition 2000
Copyright © by the University of Michigan 1998
All rights reserved
Published in the United States of America by
The University of Michigan Press
Manufactured in the United States of America
⊗ Printed on acid-free paper

2003   2002   2001   2000   5   4   3   2

A CIP catalog record for this book is available from the British Library.

Library of Congress Cataloging-in-Publication Data

Gramlich, Edward M.
    Is it time to reform social security? / Edward M. Gramlich.
      p.   cm.
    Includes bibliographical references and index.
    ISBN 0-472-09679-6 (acid-free paper) — ISBN 0-472-06679-X (pbk.
  : acid-free paper)
    1. Social security—United States—History.   2. Social security—
  United States—Forecasting.   I. Title.
  HD7125.G7   1998
  368.4'3'00973—dc21   97-45416
                                                          CIP

To our children and grandchildren
Sarah and Timothy
Robert, Meredith, and Rachel

Contents

Preface

In the middle of 1994, Social Security was a vague abstraction to me. I knew it was a large program, but as an economist I had never studied it. I knew it was there for my own retirement, but as a contributor had not a clue about the benefits I, or my family, would get in the event of my retirement, disability, or early death.

Then came a fateful telephone call that changed my life. I was asked to chair a committee I had not even heard of—the Quadrennial Advisory Council on Social Security. It turned out that the last "quadrennial" (occurring every four years) council to have studied the nation's retirement programs in depth was the 1983 council chaired by Alan Greenspan (later I was to become his colleague on the Federal Reserve Board). I had heard of the 1983 Greenspan Commission, as had most economists and many others, and had thought that the Greenspan Commission had pretty much fixed any problems there were with Social Security. While that was true at the time, I later learned about some powerful demographic and economic trends, described in the following pages, working in the other direction.

Our council was appointed and began meeting monthly in the summer of 1994. It contained thirteen members, representing unions, business, small business, pension systems, political parties, regions, and the like. We had a staff, originally directed by

David Lindeman; we appointed technical panels, chaired by Olivia Mitchell, Joseph Quinn, and Howard Young; and we had contacts in the government, mainly with Lawrence Thompson, then of the Social Security Administration, and Steven Goss, the actuary assigned to us. Each of these people served well beyond the call of duty and deserves the council's undying gratitude. We met for two and a half years and issued our report in January 1997. Our early meetings were quite amicable, but as our deliberations proceeded, some clear divisions developed and our meetings became more "strategic." While our report raised many interesting ideas and received a huge amount of attention, I felt a bit tied down trying to reconcile competing views. This book takes a different tack— here I say things my own way.

While our views will probably always differ, I have benefited from the views of other council members, forged in many, many debates. Discussions with council members Robert Ball, Sylvester Schieber, and Carolyn Weaver have strongly influenced the way I think about Social Security. Other members who have helped forge my views, perhaps to a slightly lesser degree because their own views are not so strongly held, are Edith Fierst, Thomas Jones, and Marc Twinney. Others on the staff or the technical panels, or just "hanging around" the issue, with whom I have had fruitful discussions are Henry Aaron, William Beeman, Barry Bosworth, Gary Burtless, Paul Courant, Peter Diamond, Steven Goss, Timothy Kelley, Lawrence Kotlikoff, David Lindeman, Olivia Mitchell, Alicia Munnell, Joseph Quinn, Robert Reischauer, John Shoven, Joel Slemrod, Eugene Steuerle, Lawrence Thompson, Daniel Wartonick, and Marina Whitman. There are many others, but I have to draw a line somewhere. Each made me pause and reconsider on more than one occasion.

The actual manuscript benefited enormously from the careful reading of Steven Goss, Estelle James, Joyce Manchester, Joseph Quinn, Catherine Shaw, and my wife, Ruth, who always makes telling and insightful comments. The University of Michigan Press has been very supportive and incredibly easy to work with. I remain devoted to Ruth, who has agreeably put up with a husband even more preoccupied than is normally the case (which is saying a lot!) throughout this whole Social Security experience. And my granddaughter Rachel helped immeasurably as well, by alertly listening to Grandpa's diatribes on our salutary walks in Rock Creek Park after difficult council meetings. At the time Rachel was less than a year old, but, unlike other council members, she fully agreed with Grandpa's views.

1

Mending,
but Not Ending,
Social Security

Social Security is now the federal government's largest spending program. In fiscal year 1996 it paid nearly $350 billion in benefits to 44 million people. It also taxed another 141 million workers 12.4 percent of their pay (counting both the employer and employee tax) up to a maximum amount. This tax raised $414 billion, more revenue than all other federal taxes but the personal income tax.

The program was first enacted in 1935, more than sixty years ago. While coverage has built up gradually, at this point 96 percent of the workforce is covered, and it is probably only a matter of time before workforce coverage becomes universal. The coverage among aged individuals should still be less than universal, because Social Security has always been, and is likely to remain, a program tied to labor force participation—workers have to make payroll contributions for forty quarters over their lifetime before they can qualify for benefits. But still, since Social Security also covers disabled individuals and the families of those workers suffering early death, more than 90 percent of the aged now receive benefits, and this one source provides more than 40 percent of the cash income of the aged. It would be hard to think of a program of so much importance to so many people.

Social Security also serves as the nation's most extensive insurance program. It contains many important social protections,

protections that often go underappreciated because they are taken for granted. There is redistribution within Social Security, to give low-wage workers a decent standard of living in their retirement years. For most of these low-wage workers Social Security comprises the bulk of their retirement income, and as a consequence, Social Security is far and away the nation's most effective antipoverty program. Social Security also gives financial protection to the families of workers who die early in their working career. There is financial protection against work disabilities. Social Security contains a spouse's benefit that, when combined with survivor's and disability benefits, keeps many aged widows out of poverty and makes Social Security also the nation's most important government program affecting women.

And, Social Security is also the nation's most important hedge against inflation. For many years now Social Security benefits have been fully indexed for inflation, meaning that they are automatically increased as consumer prices rise. While many private pension payments are periodically upgraded to cover past price rises, these upgrades are usually less than in proportion to the price rise, and they are usually at the discretion of the relevant employer. Social Security is virtually the only pension program in the United States with automatic proportionate inflation protection. This means that as retirees age into their nineties, as more and more are doing these days, Social Security forms their main bulwark against the gradual erosion in living standards because of inflation.

At the political level too, Social Security has proved uniquely popular. Poll after poll has confirmed its popularity, especially among the aged. Politicians know Social Security as the third rail of American politics—"touch it and you die."[1] The program is so large, pervasive, and well accepted that one almost never hears it mentioned in political campaigns or on presidential reform agendas. Social Security is taken for granted, saluted by politicians from both parties, right up there with motherhood and apple pie.

If President Roosevelt and the others responsible for the passage of the Social Security program back in 1935 had been able to look ahead sixty years, they would surely be very proud. Here is a program that has served the country well over a very long period of time, has grown hugely, has created a pervasive set of social protections, has been kept financially sound, has provided a decent return on the financial contributions of most Americans, and has been uniquely popular. How could any single program have accomplished so much?

If all this is right with Social Security, what could be the problem? Why are so many people now talking about changing this highly successful program? Why write a book with this title? To answer these questions, it is necessary to look ahead.

Changing Times

Social Security is set up as a pay-as-you-go (PAYG) system in which the current payroll taxes of workers go into a trust fund, and then the trust fund turns around and pays most of the money out in the form of benefits to current retirees. Such a system can work very well when a nation's labor force and its real wages are growing rapidly.[2] In the United States right after World War II they were. The United States came out of World War II with rapidly growing population, labor force, and real wages. This was the time of the baby boom population spurt, and a time when the United States had a near worldwide monopoly in many important manufacturing industries.

With both the size and real wages of the U.S. labor force rising rapidly, the history of the 1950s, 1960s, and 1970s was that of a gradual expansion of Social Security. New sectors of the workforce were brought into the system, disability insurance was added, and inflation protection was made explicit. Payroll tax rates did have to be raised to pay for these expansions, but these payroll tax rates were still kept very low by world standards, and generally speaking, the trust fund was in good financial health. The tradition arose of making actuarial forecasts of the balances of the trust fund 75 years in advance, and even by this strict standard, the trust fund was generally in long-term balance. Moreover, detailed financial calculations indicate that most workers born before 1935 have gotten a decent return on their payroll tax contributions. When these hard-nosed economic facts are combined with the large-scale popularity of Social Security's social protections, it is no wonder that Social Security has been popular, and has grown into a very significant program.

But this situation is changing. For one thing, the huge population growth spurt right after World War II, reflected in the so-called baby boom generation, proved to be temporary. While the baby boomers were the largest population cohort to that time in American history, they and their immediate elders did not reproduce at the same rate. Beginning in the late 1960s, American fertility rates dropped sharply. The American population is now aging, and it is only a matter of time before America's population and workforce stop growing altogether. While this was happening, people began living longer and costing the system more in their retirement years. And, U.S. economic growth rates dropped as well. Whereas the latter half of the twentieth century saw rises in Social Security benefits with low payroll tax rates, as demographers and economists peer into the twenty-first century, they see just the reverse—now the Social Security trust funds are in long-term financial imbalance, and cuts in benefits, rises in payroll tax rates, and drops in the financial returns most Americans receive on their Social Security contributions are in prospect.

Presumably most Americans would like to retain the important social protections of Social Security, but now that can only be done at a price—by making the program less attractive financially for the broad mass of Americans. And, presumably, less popular politically. Already we see age differences in the confidence that benefits will be paid. Most older Americans are still very confident that Social Security will be there to pay their benefits, but younger Americans are much less so.[3] Groups such as the Third Millennium parade the land arguing for changes in the system. Perhaps the crowning blow came in 1995 when a poll by the newspaper *USA Today* reported that more young Americans thought they would at some point see a UFO than would ever collect their Social Security benefits.

The United States does not operate in isolation but is part of an increasingly integrated world financial community. And change is in the air abroad as well. During the twentieth century there was a rush of countries into PAYG systems roughly similar to that of the United States—indeed, the United States was something of a laggard in this rush, being the twelfth developed country to adopt a social-security program. Now, around the world most countries are facing an aging population and slowing population growth, and many are facing very high current and future payroll tax rates to pay the benefits they could earlier afford with much lower tax rates. Just as the United States may have to modify its PAYG system, so may other countries. And many are—Chile, Australia, and the United Kingdom have already made major changes in their pension systems, and many other countries are seriously considering similar changes. The World Bank, among others, has also begun a campaign to get countries to reform their social-security systems.[4]

A New Approach

This book advocates some changes in Social Security policy. Since it tries to preserve what is good in the existing system but still requires significant change, I label the approach "mending, but not ending, Social Security."

The approach tries to achieve four goals.

1. Preserving the important social protections now present in Social Security

2. Bringing the trust fund that pays Social Security benefits into long-term financial solvency, for 75 years and more

3. Making Social Security economically affordable to the nation as a whole

4. Improving the financial return workers get on their Social Security contributions

It is hard to question any of these goals. Surely almost everybody would like to have affordable social protections, along with decent financial returns. While there are policies that can deal with any one of the goals, or perhaps even two or three, it is hard to find policies that can accomplish all four goals simultaneously. That is why a new approach is needed.

But there is such an approach. Somehow or other the system must move away from the PAYG system to one where there is more prefunding of benefits. Prefunded accounts represent new national saving, permitting the nation to build up its capital stock, raise future output levels, and more easily afford the higher benefit levels in prospect for the twenty-first century. These accounts can be invested either in stocks or bonds, both of which pay higher rates of return than those implicit in a PAYG system.[5] The new saving and the higher returns then permit future benefits to be afforded without higher payroll taxes.

Suppose, for example, the United States adopted the following type of program, taken from the recent report of the Quadrennial Advisory Council on Social Security.[6] On one side, the future growth of benefits for high-wage workers would be curtailed. This curtailment could be done gradually over time, without hurting any present retirees, and without jeopardizing any present important social protections. It could be done enough to limit overall pension spending costs without payroll tax increases, and enough to preserve the long-term balances of the trust funds that finance Social Security.

Coupled with that, the United States would introduce new mandatory individual accounts. These individual accounts would be the device to prefund future benefits for younger workers. They would be responsible for new national saving, leading to a stronger economy in the twenty-first century when the baby boomers begin retiring. They could be invested in packages of stock or bond funds, with higher returns than are now available in a PAYG system. They could also be operated like other centrally managed defined-contribution accounts, giving the fund managers choice among a variety of stock and bond mutual funds, and individual owners choices of different packages of these funds.

The key part of the plan is the new individual accounts. Prefunding does not have to be done through individual accounts—an alternative method would be to simply raise payroll taxes in advance of future benefits. But as long as the payroll taxes would finance the central trust fund, there are serious difficulties (discussed below) in having these public funds invested in the stock market, so the investment possibilities of payroll tax generated prefunding are very limited. In addition, it is likely that contributions to individual accounts would be a more popular way to raise overall national saving than widely scorned payroll tax increases.

That is the message of this book. Prefunding of future benefits should be done, somehow or other. It should be done in a way that raises overall national saving, to give the overall economy the capital resources to help pay for rising future benefit costs. There are different ways of prefunding benefits, but the economic and political possibilities seem most promising if the prefunding is done through individual accounts that are combined with Social Security. Older retirees escape cuts in benefits, and younger workers gain the stronger future economy and greater returns on their contributions. If the package is enacted fairly soon, it should be possible to preserve all the important social protections of Social Security and still give most workers of most ages decent returns on their payroll contributions. Social Security can indeed be mended, but not ended.

2

Social Security
in the
Twentieth Century

In 1935 President Franklin Roosevelt signed into law the Social Security Act. This act marked the introduction of broad-scale social-insurance programs in the United States, following the earlier introduction of similar programs in eleven European countries. The Social Security system did not develop into its modern form until the 1950s, but since then it has grown into a huge, and hugely popular, program. By fiscal 1996 44 million people were receiving benefits totaling $347 billion (22 percent of all federal spending); and 141 million workers (96 percent of the workforce) were paying payroll taxes totaling $414 billion. Because Social Security pays so many benefits to so many people, few politicians are willing to tamper with it.

While most older Americans take Social Security's popularity as an act of faith, younger Americans may be getting restless. Current-day Social Security Trustees' Reports indicate that the assets of the trust funds that finance Social Security, the Old Age, Survivors, and Disability Trust Funds (OASDI), will be exhausted by year 2029, before many working Americans will retire.[1] Polling data report big age differences in respondents' confidence that benefits will be available, and influential books are written against Social Security.[2] Five of the thirteen members of President Clinton's 1996 Advisory Council on Social Security came out in favor of a very radical restructuring plan.[3] And many Latin American and European countries have already undertaken radical restructuring plans of their own.

Is it time to drastically reform the U.S. Social Security system? This book argues for some change, but not for dramatic change. The argument is given in the next five chapters. This chapter describes the historical evolution of Social Security. Of all the ways the system could have evolved, why did it evolve as it did, and how does it now work? The third chapter describes the Social Security problem, which is really not a current problem at all but one anticipated for the twenty-first century. The fourth chapter discusses the goals of Social Security reform. The fifth chapter compares many potential solutions to Social Security's anticipated problem and shows (at least in my view) that only my approach meets all the important goals of Social Security reform. The last chapter describes approaches many other countries are taking to reform their Social Security systems, largely for the same reasons that the U.S. must reform its system.

Prefunding, Defined Benefits, and Defined Contributions

When the politicians of the 1930s were debating Social Security, they made a number of important decisions. These decisions may have been right for the 1930s, and they have certainly stood the test of time. But today's world is very different from that of the 1930s, and tomorrow's world will be even more different. So it seems like a reasonable time to reexamine some of these important historical decisions.

The most fundamental decisions involved the financing of the program. President Roosevelt himself argued for a program that was contributory and largely prefunded, with payroll taxes going into a dedicated trust fund and generating later retirement benefits. Roosevelt argued against any general-revenue financing for these old-age insurance benefits because he felt that general-revenue financing would turn social insurance into social assistance. Then and now there did exist a general-revenue-financed old-age assistance program, now known as Supplemental Security Income (SSI). On what might be considered the political left of Roosevelt's preferred program was the Townsend plan, a noncontributory universal assistance program recommended by a Dr. Townsend of California but rejected by the Congress. On the political right was a voluntary program proposed by Senator Bennet Clark of Missouri, and also rejected by the Congress.[4] While the Congress disposed of both issues back then, these same issues have continued to arise throughout the history of Social Security.

As the program passed in the 1930s developed into the 1950s, it evolved into a contributory payroll tax system financed by a dedicated trust fund. The contributory part means that the only workers who get benefits are those who have paid into the trust fund, with benefits depending in some way on past payroll contributions. Taxes are paid into the dedicated trust fund and benefits are paid out. But for political reasons it has never proved possible to build up a sizable fund reserve—that would have required taxes far in excess of benefits. This means that the trust fund has essentially operated on what is known as a PAYG basis, with present-day payroll taxes from workers paying benefits for retirees who had previously paid payroll taxes.

Since Social Security benefits are determined by a set of rules relating benefits to a worker's past earnings, Social Security is also said to be a defined-benefit (DB) pension plan. Were benefits instead determined by the actual accumulations from past worker contributions, the program would be considered a defined-contribution (DC) plan. By their very nature DC plans are prefunded, while DB plans may or may not be.[5] But Roosevelt's desired reserve has never been built up, and the U.S. Social Security DB plan has never been prefunded to any significant degree.

Throughout the 1950s, 1960s, and 1970s benefit levels were gradually increased, partly to adjust for rises in living costs and partly reflecting real programmatic expansions. Coverage was expanded also, and now Social Security is nearly universal. It covers 96 percent of the workforce, all but a small share of state and local workers who have been permitted to remain outside the system because of perceived Constitutional reasons. It pays benefits to 91 percent of the aged.

Payroll tax rates have then been raised as needed to keep the program on a PAYG basis, with the payroll taxes always evenly shared between employers and employees.[6] The combined payroll tax rate for employers and employees began at 2 percent (1 percent on each) on wages up to $3,000 in 1937, rose to 3 percent (1.5 percent on each) on wages up to $3,600 by 1951, and in 1997 was 10.52 percent (5.26 percent on each) on wages up to $65,400 for the old-age insurance program alone. A disability insurance program was added with its own trust fund and payroll tax in 1956—now the combined payroll tax for disability insurance is 1.88 percent on wages up to $65,400 (making for an OASDI combined payroll tax rate of 12.4 percent, 6.2 percent apiece on employers and employees). Medicare was added in 1965, financed by its own payroll tax (now another 2.9 percent combined payroll tax, on all wages) and with benefits paid by its own trust fund. While for many purposes Medicare might be analyzed alongside Social Security, in this book I look mainly at the OASDI system, only bringing in Medicare when it is particularly relevant.

The only real break in the PAYG tradition occurred in the mid-1980s, when as a feature of the Social Security compromise of that time, payroll taxes were raised somewhat in advance of the impending rise in benefits. This partial advance funding has led to some accumulation of reserves for the combined OASDI trust fund, now about a year and a half's worth of benefit payments. This reserve fund is not nearly large enough to prefund benefits, but it represents some movement in the direction originally desired by President Roosevelt.

The Determination of Social Security Benefits

The benefit formula that underlies Social Security is based on workers' past earnings. It is designed to establish a balance between social adequacy—giving low-wage workers a livable benefit level in their retirement—and individual equity—providing a decent return on the contributions of all workers, including high-wage workers.

The payrolls that workers and their employers have paid taxes on are computed as if the wages were earned in the year the worker turned 60, to adjust for growth in the average wage level in the economy. They are then averaged for the highest 35 years in the worker's career, to smooth out ups and downs in wage earnings.

The actual benefits given by this procedure for a single worker in 1996 are shown in table 2.1. The left column gives the taxable wages, assumed to be averaged over 35 years and then expressed in 1996 dollars. Using Social Security Administration (SSA) data and classifications, low-wage workers are those who earn (and pay payroll taxes on) about $10,000 per year. Average-wage workers earn about $30,000 per year. High-wage workers earn closer to $40,000 per year, and maximum-wage workers earn about $60,000 per year. All workers earning more than $65,400 per year would be assessed payroll taxes only on their first $65,400, so they too would be considered to be maximum-wage workers by the SSA.

The benefit formula determines a quantity known as the Primary Insurance Amount (PIA), shown in the middle column. This PIA is generally the worker's basic benefit if the worker retires at the normal retirement age, which is now 65.[7] The social-adequacy goal is reflected in the fact that low-wage workers get $6,242 per year at age 65, not enough to keep these workers out of poverty without some other income, but still a relatively good return on their contributions. That is reflected in the high value for what is known as the replacement rate, shown in the right column and calculated here by dividing the PIA by average taxable wages.[8]

The individual equity goal is shown by the fact that as we move down the table to workers of higher wage income, who have paid in more, benefits in the form of the PIA rise. But the increases are less than proportionate. Hence maximum wage workers get $17,417 in benefits at age 65, but their replacement rate is only 29 percent. If replacement rates were computed on the wages of workers earning more than $60,000, they would be even lower—17 percent for workers earning $100,000, and so forth.

Since the past wages on which workers have paid payroll taxes are brought up to date and computed as if they were earned the year the worker turned 60, these benefits are said to be wage indexed (automatically inflated at the rate of growth of taxable wages in the economy). Once workers become eligible for retire-

TABLE 2.1. Primary Insurance Amounts (PIA) and Replacement Rates in Relation to Averaged Indexed Taxable Wages for Single Workers Who Turned 62 in 1996 (annual rates)

Taxable Wage ($)	PIA ($)	Replacement Rate (%)
10,000	6,242	62
20,000	9,442	47
30,000	12,642	42
40,000	14,417	36
50,000	15,917	32
60,000	17,417	29

ment, their benefits are price indexed (automatically inflated at the rate of increase of the consumer price index, or CPI). In 1996 a special congressional committee of economists reported that the CPI was biased on the high side by about 1.1 percentage points a year.[9] Were the price-indexing formula to be altered to reflect all or part of this bias, there would be no impact whatever on the numbers in table 2.1, which are in no way influenced by the CPI. But there would be an impact on those who have already retired and have begun receiving their Social Security benefits, because these benefits would not rise so much over time. Such a change could have an enormous impact on the next century's very old, who would have been retired a long time.

The technical name for the normal retirement age is the age at which workers are first eligible for their full benefits, those shown in table 2.1.[10] Workers are first eligible for retirement benefits at age 62, though these benefits are reduced for all succeeding retirement years. The reductions are calculated so that workers on average do not gain from retiring early. Currently workers receive about 80 percent of the numbers shown in table 2.1 if they retire at age 62. Workers can also work past age 65 and receive what is known as a delayed retirement credit. This credit is now being gradually enhanced so that soon it will nearly be a matter of financial indifference, to the average worker and to the OASDI trust funds, whether the worker retires at any age between 62 and 70.[11]

The Social Security changes passed in the mid-1980s will gradually increase the normal retirement age. It is 65 now, and in year 2000 it begins increasing by two months per year, so that it becomes 66 in year 2005. Then it stays at 66 for twelve years—a period known as the hiatus—before advancing again by two months a year between years 2017 and 2022. It will become 67 for workers reaching age 62 in year 2022. One thing not generally understood about Social Security is that these changes are already scheduled in present law—if one proposes raising the normal retirement age to improve the system's finances, that proposal must involve raising the age more than in the above schedule. But the already-enacted changes in the normal retirement age still make it possible to retire at age 62, with greater benefit reductions. This means that workers who retire at age 62 after 2021 will get something like 70 percent of the benefits described in table 2.1, and indeed that workers retiring at any constant age (62, 63, etc.) will get actuarially reduced benefits. This is why analysts who talk about Social Security usually consider changes in the normal retirement age as proportionate cuts in Social Security benefits. But they are really proportionate cuts only for workers young enough to be affected by the changes.

Social Security also includes what is known as a spouse's benefit. The benefit for a nonworking spouse married to the worker at least 10 years is 50 percent of the worker's PIA. When this spouse has also worked for at least 10 years in covered work, SSA will give him or her the larger of the spouse benefit or the benefit based on the worker's own earnings record. While in the past most aged women have received benefits based on their husbands' earning records, the SSA projects that in the future the rise in female workforce participation will alter the situation—most aged women will be on their own earnings record. Surviving spouse benefits are also available, generally the higher of the deceased spouse PIA or that worker's own PIA.[12]

Since the mid-1950s, Social Security has also included protection against work-related disabilities. There is a rather complicated screening procedure to determine eligibility, but if workers are deemed eligible, they are entitled to their PIA, computed from their years of work until their disablement. This means that changes in the normal retirement age do not change benefits for disabled workers. Presently only a small percentage of the workforce, about 3 percent, receives Social Security disability benefits.[13]

Since the mid-1980s, Social Security benefits have been taxable under the federal personal income tax. The question of exactly how Social Security benefits should be taxed is very complicated. Workers have already paid federal personal income taxes on their own wages, but their employers have not, since employers can deduct their payroll contributions in computing their taxable profits. Under normal income tax procedures for taxing private DB pension plans, all benefits in excess of previously taxed employee contributions are taxable, a standard that would imply including of about 85 percent of Social Security benefits in the taxable incomes for most retirees. Roughly, this is the present tax situation. But there are still some deviations from comparable tax treatment. One is that Social Security benefits are only taxable when total income, including Social Security, is above some special thresholds—thresholds that are not available for other DB pension plans. Another deviation is that the revenue from these taxes does not go to the general Treasury, but rather is split between the OASDI Trust Funds and the Medicare Trust Fund, with the revenue available to fund future benefits in both programs. To say the least, it would be strange if the revenue from the taxation of private pension income were made available to fund future private pension payments.

The Impact on the Poor and Women

While Social Security was not explicitly designed as a program to help either poor people or women, the program operates in a way that is a huge boost to both groups.

As was shown in table 2.1 above, in an attempt to preserve social adequacy the Social Security benefit received by a typical low-wage single worker is in the neighborhood of $6,000 annually. By itself, this benefit is not enough to keep this worker out of poverty. Yet if the worker collects the spouse benefit, or if the spouse has also been a worker and collects even more than the spouse benefit, or if the worker or couple has some other outside income, the couple should be out of poverty. Simple calculations based on the incomes of the poor show that removing Social Security benefits would add about 15 million older people to the ranks of the poor. The true impact of Social Security on poverty is undoubtedly less than this because without Social Security many aged poor would still be working. But Social Security is still far and away the nation's most significant antipoverty program.[14]

Another way to look at the situation is shown in figure 2.1. The figure gives the shares of aggregate income for aged family units, broken down by income quintiles. The pie chart in the top left shows the share of aggregate income received by the bottom fifth of aged family units, those with incomes below $6,939 in 1992 (or about $7,760 in 1996, slightly above the poverty line). These poor or near-poor family units receive a whopping 81 percent of their cash income from Social Security, with only a minuscule 13 percent coming from private pensions and virtually nothing from work. As we move up in the scale, Social Security becomes progressively less important—77 percent of the income for the next quintile, and on down to 20 percent of the income for the top quintile. Viewed in this light, Social Security is very important in supporting incomes for those at the bottom of the income scale.

Poverty is high in America, and Social Security cannot cure, or at least has not cured, poverty all by itself. But it has done a decent job, as shown in figure 2.2. This figure gives aggregate poverty rates—the share of individuals in the relevant class living in poverty—by age in year 1992. Overall, 14 percent of Americans were in poverty status in that year. The poorest overall group is children, where 22 percent of American children were growing up in poverty. This is an often-noted phenomenon, and a very regret-

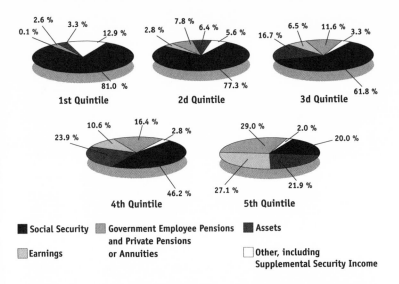

FIGURE 2.1. Sources of income of aged family units 65 or older, by quintiles of total money income, 1992. Quintile limits are $6,939, $11,226, $17,645, $29,052. (Calculations based on data from *Income of the Aged: 1992* [Washington, DC: Social Security Administration].)

table one—would that Social Security could cure it. But it cannot—to the extent that Social Security has an impact, it is on the aged, and here we see that the aggregate poverty rate for those over 65 was about 12 percent, below the national average. The aged poverty rate would be far above the national average without the 80 percent of the income of these groups that comprises Social Security benefits.

One lamentable aspect of poverty even among the aged is that poverty rates do creep up for women, especially those over 75. Figure 2.2 shows poverty rates for women over 75 of nearly 20 percent. As with the other aged groups, these poverty rates would be far higher were it not for the spouse benefit of Social Security, the

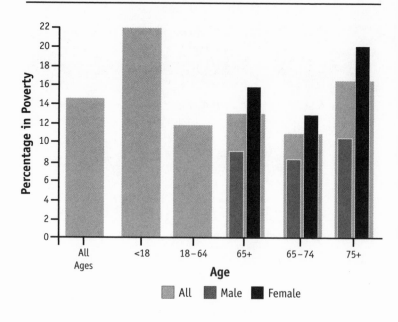

FIGURE 2.2. Poverty rates by age and sex, 1992. (From Bureau of the Census 1993, tables 2, 3, and 5.)

survivor's protection, and the inflation protection, which matters significantly for the oldest of the aged. But many poverty scholars argue that the United States could do much better, even within the present structure of Social Security. Instead of the current practice of paying surviving spouses the highest workers' PIA, a simple change would give the surviving spouse 75 percent of the amount received by the couple before one of the members died, approximately matching the reduction in cost of living once one member dies. This simple change, balanced by a slight cut in the spouse benefit, would lower aged widow poverty rates by about 5 percentage points, bringing these down to at least the overall national average poverty rate.[15]

A Compulsory System

When Social Security was first being debated, Senator Clark of Missouri proposed exempting workers for firms that already had their own pension plans. The Clark amendment was voted down, and to this day Social Security has been a compulsory system. Why?

There are several good reasons. Since there is redistribution within Social Security, high-income workers do not get as good a financial deal as low-income workers—they get lower replacement rates (see table 2.1) and lower returns on their contributions (to be shown in the next chapter). If they were given the option to leave the system, there would be fewer funds there to support low-income workers, and the cost of this support for the remaining workers would rise. Rather than being a universal program that covers all Americans, Social Security would gradually turn into a welfare program only covering low-wage workers, and providing much higher cost social insurance for these workers. It would also be more vulnerable politically, as high-income workers would have less reason to support it.

Another dimension of this issue involves saving. Social Security can be thought of as a mandatory pension saving plan for workers. It could, of course, be argued that workers should be able to look ahead and save for themselves. But that is hard for workers to do, when they do not know how long they will live, how long their spouses will live, and how much resources their family will need in retirement years. Sometimes it makes sense to have the government help with such decisions, by forcing workers to put aside a certain amount while working, and by providing benefits that are automatically adjusted for inflation for as long as the worker, or the worker's family, lives. Without such help, workers would be likely to undersave.[16]

While Social Security may be getting more costly and may be in need of some change, very few commentators are actually suggesting that Social Security be made into a voluntary system. There can be ways to introduce more individual responsibility into the system, but the dominant view is that all Americans should be part of the system. That is also why one of the least controversial recommendations of the otherwise divided 1996 advisory council is that all new workers should be brought into the system at the earliest opportunity.[17]

Actuarial Soundness

Being a DB plan, Social Security is set up with an elaborate review system. Every year the trustees of Social Security, three cabinet officers, the commissioner of SSA, and two outside members, produce a Trustees' Report that computes the actuarial soundness of the OASDI trust funds for the next 75 years. Periodically these Trustees' Reports are buttressed by outside advisory councils that comment on the reasonableness of the trustees' assumptions and calculations, and also make policy suggestions. These reports ask whether under reasonable economic and demographic assumptions, the trust funds can pay the benefits projected under current law, and described above. While the long-term finances of the trust funds looked sound back in the mid-1980s, the last time a thorough advisory council assessment was made, they may not look so sound now. The next chapter goes into details.

3

Social Security
in the
Twenty-first Century

The Social Security system that has evolved over the latter half of the twentieth century could be continued on into the twenty-first century. But given the major demographic, economic, and sociological changes in the United States, such a continuation would mean steadily higher payroll tax rates on workers and steadily lower financial returns on the money workers have paid in to qualify for their benefits. What could happen then is not necessarily the best thing to happen. In this chapter I review the forecasts for the present system into the twenty-first century, as if the present benefit system were continued intact. In succeeding chapters we get to the new policy options.

Forecasting

Traditionally Social Security forecasts have been made 75 years into the future. Given the glacial but significant changes in many demographic variables, it is certainly worthwhile to look this far ahead. At the same time, we should not delude ourselves about the accuracy of any such set of forecasts—it is as if a group of demographers and economists in the Harding administration were attempting to forecast key variables for society now.

The SSA does what it can to assure the reasonableness of the forecasts. The forecasters make three different forecasts—for an intermediate-cost (or best-guess) scenario, a high-cost scenario, and a low-cost scenario. Every year the Trustees' Report updates these 75-year forecast scenarios. Their assumptions about demographic and economic trends are made public, and discussed and debated by outside scholars. Then periodic outside advisory councils appoint technical panels, made up of other outside demographers, economists, and sociologists, to review the accuracy of the assumptions made for these long-term forecasts.[1]

There has been some tendency for the forecasts to be on the optimistic side. In the extensive Social Security revisions of 1983, for example, the forecast numbers did prove to be optimistic, and they had to be, and were, revised in the direction of greater realism (and greater actuarial deficits) for all the reports on Social Security in the 1990s.[2] While recognizing this uncertainty, and the fact that things may not turn out as well as forecast, in the following analysis I use the very latest forecasts of the outlook for Social Security, made by the trustees in the spring of 1997.[3] To the extent that these forecasts turn out to be optimistic, most of my later policy arguments can be made that much more forcefully.

The Baby Boom

Given normal patterns of sickness and mortality, if every woman had 2.1 babies in her lifetime, the overall population of a country would stabilize. A fertility rate above 2.1 would lead to natural population growth; one less than 2.1 would lead the natural population to decline eventually. This simple rule is complicated by factors such as immigration and changes in life expectancy, which could generate overall population increases or decreases at fertility rates slightly different from 2.1. But even in a country with as much immigration and changes in life expectancy as the United States, these complications are not major, and a fertility rate of 2.1 is approximately the zero-population-growth fertility rate for the United States.

The actual pattern of U.S. total fertility rates,[4] past and projected, is shown in figure 3.1. The general pattern shown there is very common for developed countries around the world. Back in the nineteenth century U.S. fertility rates were well above 2.1 but were declining. That gradual decline continued to 1920, at which time fertility rates took a sharp drop, arriving at the magical level of 2.1 in the depression year of 1930. Had fertility rates continued at their level of the 1930s, the overall U.S. population growth rate would have been low in the years following World War II, and it would be approximately zero by now.

But that is not what happened. Following World War II U.S. fertility rates took a remarkable leap, creating a population cohort now known as the baby boom generation. Technically, baby boomers are those born between 1946 and 1964, though a close examination of figure 3.1 indicates that if this boom were defined relative to the magical 2.1 number, it should be extended a few years on both ends. The presumptive reasons for the baby boom are well known—the period following World War II was one of great optimism, families were moving to the suburbs where land was cheap and living space plentiful, incomes were rising rapidly, mothers generally stayed home and raised families, divorce rates were low, and there was then little of the present-day talk about limits to growth. Because overall population was generally rising before the baby boom, this generation of Americans is the largest to that time in American history. Because the baby boomers themselves have had fertility rates below the magic 2.1 number, and because this low fertility is projected to continue, the baby boom generation is also likely to be the largest in American history from now on.

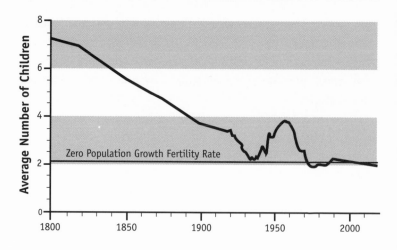

FIGURE 3.1. U.S. total fertility rates, 1800–2020. Data before 1920 for whites only, adjusted to equal the fertility rate for all races in 1920. (Historical data from National Center for Health Statistics; projected data from Social Security and Medicare Boards of Trustees 1997.)

Working out all the implications of the baby boom on American society is like watching a snake swallow a fish. In the 1950s the baby boom meant enormous expenditures on houses and schools, in the 1960s it meant rapid growth in spending on higher education, in the 1970s it meant a rapid growth in the labor force, and in the twenty-first century it will mean a rapid growth in the number of people needing to be supported by Social Security.

Expected Lifetimes

The other relevant demographic fact is that people are living longer. In 1935 when the Social Security system was first started the overall life expectancy at birth was 61 years. More than half of all Americans would not even live to collect their Social Security benefits (though their families might collect survivor benefits). Now average life expectancy at birth is 75 years for men, 78 years for women. In the twenty-first century it is projected to rise to 80 years and over for both groups.

It is perhaps more meaningful to measure life expectancy at age 65, the period that corresponds with costs for the OASDI system. These numbers, for men and women under the three scenarios, are shown in figure 3.2. In 1935 new male retirees would be alive, and receiving benefits, for an average of 12 years, new female retirees for 13 years. By now the numbers have increased to 15 and 18 years respectively, implying OASDI cost increases of about 30 percent from this source alone. In the twenty-first century these costs are projected to continue rising, because of secular increases in life expectancy.

Social Security Finances

The projected implications of both of these trends on Social Security's demographics are shown in figure 3.3. As was noted earlier, Social Security is now basically a PAYG system in which present-day workers provide benefits for present-day retirees. Back in 1950 there were 16 workers to pay the benefits of the 1950 retirees. By 1960, when the system had evolved into its modern form, the number had dropped to 5 workers per beneficiary. By 1997 economic and demographic trends had dropped the number to 3.3 workers per beneficiary. In some sense present-day workers have to pay fifty percent more than 1960 workers (the inverse of 3.3 divided by the inverse of 5) to provide benefits for today's retirees. By the year 2008, when the oldest baby boomers begin

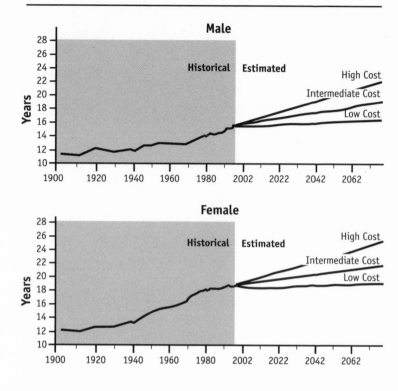

FIGURE 3.2. Life expectancy at age 65. (Historical data from National Center for Health Statistics; projected data from Social Security and Medicare Boards of Trustees 1997.)

retiring, the number is projected to be 3.0 (under the best-guess scenario). By 2030, when the youngest baby boomers retire, the number is projected to be down to 2.0. Workers in 2030 are projected to have to pay two and a half times as much as 1960 workers to provide retirement benefits. And after that, the ratio is projected to get even more unfavorable, as people continue to live longer and the population continues to age. By year 2070 there are expected to be only 1.8 workers per beneficiary, and workers then will have to pay nearly three times as much as 1960 workers to provide retirement benefits.

There is productivity growth as economies develop, and it is at least theoretically possible that the underlying growth in productivity and real wages could make these benefits affordable without rises in payroll tax rates. But now comes more bad news. In the optimistic days following World War II real wage growth averaged more than 2 percent per year, implying a doubling of real wages every 35 years. Reasons for this rapid growth generally involved the conversion of military technology to civilian purposes, the fact that the United States came out of the war with a worldwide monopoly in many manufacturing industries, cheap natural resources, and the fact that environmental costs had not yet become serious (or at least not yet recognized). Beginning in the mid-1970s, the United States economy suffered what is known as a productivity slowdown, in which all of these factors turned around. Since the mid-1970s real wage growth has been under 1 percent per year, implying that it now would take a full century for real wages to double. The latest Trustees' Report, supported by the technical panel of economists, now projects the rate of real wage growth into the indefinite future at 0.9 percent per year.

While the drop in the rate of growth of real wages is not good news, the demographic trends are. The rise in life expectancies is obviously desirable. Moreover, the slowing of the rate of overall population growth, in the United States and around the world (where there are similar declines in fertility rates) is a very welcome development. It is hard to see how planet Earth could support rapidly growing numbers of people indefinitely without this decline in fertility. But while the demographic trends are most welcome, the combination of reduced fertility, rising life expectancies, and slowing real wage growth does cause major difficulties for the PAYG, defined-benefit Social Security system. The extent of the difficulties for the United States is shown in figures 3.4 and 3.5.[5]

Figure 3.4 gives what is known as an income statement for the Old Age, Survivors, and Disability Insurance Trust Funds, under present-law projections. The grayish horizontal line shows fund inflows—in effect the combined OASDI payroll tax rate, now 12.4 percent on employers and employees, and under present law slated to remain at 12.4 percent indefinitely. The solid upward sloping lines show projected fund outflows under the three scenarios. Because of the falling number of workers per beneficiary, shown in figure 3.3, the implicit payroll tax cost on workers is likely to rise.

Before analyzing these trends further, there is one issue that leads to a significant amount of confusion. It can be seen from figure 3.4 that in 1995 the OASDI trust funds were in surplus (the inflow line is higher than the outflow line). The surplus that year totaled $67 billion. This surplus is normally included in the federal budget in political discussions, but the impact of this inclusion is often misunderstood. The OASDI surplus is invested in government bonds, and the OASDI trust funds are properly credited with all interest earned on these bonds. This means that this surplus is clearly not stolen from Social Security, as one often hears in political campaigns. Since all future benefits must be paid from this fund, the OASDI trust funds also already satisfy a long-term financial constraint, provided that the long-term actuarial forecasts are in balance.

While the OASDI accounting is appropriate, an entirely separate question is whether the trust fund accounts should be included in the federal budget. In a very technical sense they are not—various budget laws force budget scorekeepers to show separately the OASDI accounts and the rest of government accounts. But for all practical purposes Congress and the administration talk about budget totals including Social Security, perhaps because the budget deficit would be $67 billion greater if that were not done. For many purposes it may be appropriate to show separately the deficit of the rest of government, which deficit is indeed larger by $67 billion, but that is not a Social Security issue.

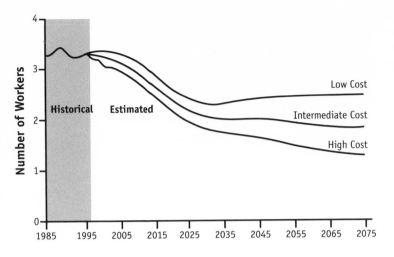

FIGURE 3.3. Number of workers per beneficiary. (From Social Security and Medicare Boards of Trustees 1997.)

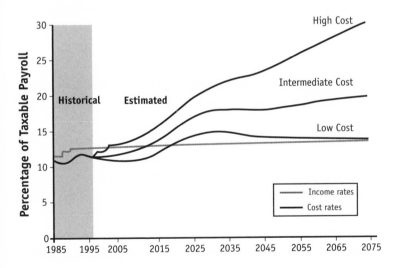

FIGURE 3.4. OASDI income rates and cost rates. (From Social Security and Medicare Boards of Trustees 1997.)

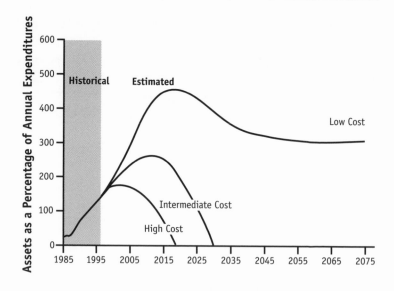

FIGURE 3.5. Trust fund ratios for OASDI trust funds. (From Social Security and Medicare Boards of Trustees 1997.)

In any case, this surplus is expected to continue until about year 2012 in the best-guess scenario (at that point the politics of including Social Security in the federal budget are likely to change dramatically!). Then, as the baby boomers begin retiring, benefit costs should rise rapidly compared to payroll tax inflows. The PAYG tax rate to balance the system, read from the outflow line, should be about 18 percent by 2035, 19 percent by 2075, and so forth. The rate of ascent is not that great after the baby boom retirement period is over, but the direction is clear, and there would have to be major unanticipated demographic or economic changes to alter this basic trend.

Figure 3.5 shows the net assets of the fund, in terms of asset stocks. These are reflected by what is known as the trust fund ratio, the ratio of net assets to annual expenditures. In 1995 this trust fund ratio was about 150 percent—meaning that if no revenues had come in at all, the trust fund could still have paid full benefits for about a year and a half. In the surplus years up to 2012, the fund should accumulate assets, and the trust fund ratio is likely to rise to a peak of a little more than 250 percent of annual expenditures. By year 2012, if no new money were to come into the trust fund, the fund should be able to pay full benefits for a little more than two and a half years. But by then the baby boomers begin retiring in force, assets are likely to be spent down at a rapid pace, and these assets are likely to be exhausted by about year 2029.

This date is the one most commonly heard about Social Security. It is easy to misinterpret, especially for those who will be retiring after 2029. What it means technically is that the accumulated assets of the trust fund are likely to be exhausted at that date. If the PAYG trust fund arrangement is continued after that time, this in turn means that Social Security benefits will not be zero, but they can be only about three-quarters as high as implied by present law (the 12.4 percent inflow divided by the 17 percent outflow shown in figure 3.4) if they are to match anticipated payroll tax inflows. There is a lot of time to change the law by then, and the present-law benefit schedule could always be financed by general revenues. Were that to happen, the diversion from the general Treasury could be measured from the financing gap between the inflow and outflow lines.

Without getting into the details of policy at this point, it is possible to use these figures to assess the magnitude of the policy changes required to bring the system into long-term actuarial balance. The past tradition has been to keep the projected trust fund ratio above 100 percent for 75 years. Were this rule to be followed now, the required payroll tax increase would be 2.2 percentage points, making the overall OASDI payroll tax rate 14.6 percent.

Using the standard forecasts, an immediate 2.2 percent payroll tax increase would in effect bend the trust fund ratio path in figure 3.5 to the northeast so that the ratio would be 100 percent (that is, the trust funds would have a year's worth of benefits on hand) in year 2075. But the trust fund ratio line would still be downward sloping in the later years of the forecast horizon because of the heavy expenses in these out-years. The sheer passage of time would then drive the system out of actuarial balance sometime after year 2075.

A stronger and more reasonable actuarial test would require that the passage of time alone not put the system out of balance. This is tantamount to requiring that the trust fund ratio in the last years of the forecast would be stable. This test would be satisfied by an immediate payroll tax increase of 3.3 percentage points, to an overall payroll tax rate of 15.7 percent.[6] This 3.3 percentage point number seems the most meaningful estimate of the present-day financial gap.

Phrasing this long-term actuarial deficit in payroll tax terms is only a statistical convenience. In fact, adjustments could be made on the benefit side as well to keep the system in long-term actuarial balance. But while either tax increases or benefit cuts could in some financial sense bring the system into long-term actuarial balance, there is another complication involving the return Social Security contributors realize on their wage payments. To this concern we now turn.

Financial Returns

One can think of a pure PAYG system in this way. Every year workers pay in a share of their payroll earnings to the OASDI trust funds, and the trust funds pay out the money in the form of benefits to present-day retirees. In a stable society, with no growth in the labor force, no growth in real wages, and everybody living until retirement, the amount of benefits that the average present-day worker would get later on when she retires is just what she paid in. In investment terms, the real return on the contributions of this worker would then be zero percent.

The fertility and mortality assumptions discussed earlier are reasonably consistent with this example, so as far as the demographic parameters are concerned, the U.S. PAYG Social Security system would approximately pay zero percent to the average worker. But real wages are assumed to be rising at the rate of 0.9 percent per year into the indefinite future in the long-term actuarial forecasts. If payroll tax rates were to be stable, this would then mean that Social Security real benefits would be growing by 0.9 percent a year, or that they would effectively yield an overall rate of return of about 0.9 percent.[7] Given the replacement rate differences shown in table 2.1, the implicit rate of return would be somewhat above 0.9 percent for low-wage workers and somewhat below 0.9 percent for high-wage workers. It would be still higher than these levels for workers that gain the spouse benefit, lower than these levels for workers that die early, and so forth.[8]

Actual real rates of return for single male workers, by various earnings levels and dates of birth, are shown in table 3.1. In computing these rates of return, the table assumes present law, though with payroll tax rates raised as needed to finance future benefits when the trust fund is exhausted (a scenario labeled present-law PAYG). Reading down any one column, say the column for workers with average earnings (about $25,000 in today's dollars), there is a steady decline. Average-wage workers born in 1920, who only paid in to Social Security for a part of their work life but received full benefits, received an implicit real return of 2.75 percent—much higher than they would get in long-term equilibrium. Workers born in 1930 will get less, 1.92 percent, and on down, so that workers not yet born will get 0.81, very close to the 0.9 percent long-term tendency. Workers with low earnings born in any year do better than this because of the redistribution in the system, and workers with higher earnings born in any year do worse, also because of the redistribution. Very young maximum-wage workers are actually slated to realize negative returns, which means that they are likely to get fewer real benefits than their real contributions.

Another way to display the same point is in terms of what SSA terms the "money's worth" of one's contributions. The money's worth ratio for any worker is the present value of all benefits received as a percentage of the present value of all contributions made, by employer and employee alike.[9] When these money's worth ratios equal 100 percent, Social Security would be returning exactly the same amount as would government bonds; when the money's worth ratios exceed 100 percent, Social Security would pay a better rate of return than would government bonds, and when the money's worth ratios are less than 100 percent, Social Security would pay a worse rate of return than would bonds. Older workers who joined the system late in their working career but

TABLE 3.1. Real Internal Rates of Return (in percent) on Single Male Worker's Accumulated Lifetime Social Security Contributions, by Worker's Year of Birth

Birthdate	Low Earnings	Average Earnings	High Earnings	Maximum Earnings
1920	4.37	2.75	2.45	2.35
1930	3.06	1.92	1.54	1.15
1937	2.66	1.59	1.15	0.66
1943	2.36	1.33	0.80	0.25
1949	2.43	1.40	0.78	0.19
1955	2.45	1.43	0.77	0.08
1964	2.37	1.33	0.66	−0.11
1973	2.32	1.26	0.58	−0.22
1985	2.16	1.10	0.42	−0.35
1997	1.95	0.92	0.25	−0.51
2004	1.83	0.81	0.16	−0.58

Source: Advisory Council on Social Security 1997.

received full benefits have gotten very high money's worth ratios on their contributions. Younger workers who paid in through their whole career and experience the low equilibrium return on contributions will get much lower money's worth ratios on their contributions.

Given that rates of return vary so much according to whether a worker has low or high earnings, claims a spouse benefit, uses disability, lives a long time or a short time, it makes sense to examine the pure impact of Social Security on composite workers born at different dates by averaging money's worth ratios and numbers of workers getting different treatment. These weighted average money's worth ratios for composite workers are shown in figure 3.6. The workers born before 1937, not shown in the figure, would have relatively high money's worth ratios. Beginning with workers born after 1937, the figure shows money's worth ratios for four different approaches to Social Security. For now we concentrate only on the line labeled PL PAYG, present law on a pay-as-you-go regime in which the payroll tax rate is raised as needed to maintain the finances of the OASDI trust funds. (The other approaches are discussed in chapter 5.)

Because the long-run rate of return on contributions for the average worker is about 0.9 percent per year, in line with the above example, and well below the real rate of return on government bonds, there is a general downward trend in money's worth ratios. They are about 100 percent for workers born in the 1930s and retiring now, and gradually descend to about 70 percent for workers born in the next century. This decline is not smooth, however, because of the historical pattern of interest rates. Workers born in the 1950s could have invested their retirement contributions in bonds paying the abnormally high real rates of returns of the 1980s—for them money's worth ratios are abnormally low, and Social Security looks like an especially bad investment.[10]

Social Security is, of course, far more than an investment. It

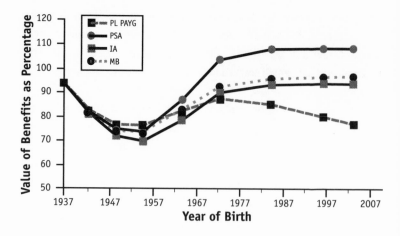

FIGURE 3.6. Present value of expected OASDI benefits as a percentage of present value of expected contributions, for composite workers, by year of birth. (From Advisory Council on Social Security 1997.)

contains social insurance against work disabilities, social insurance against both early death and against the possibility of outliving one's assets, and inflation protection. In general people cannot buy private insurance to protect against all these contingencies and might be quite willing to accept money's worth ratios of less than 100 percent as a necessary cost of their social insurance. But the fact that rates of return are steadily dropping still means that Social Security is becoming increasingly unattractive as an investment outlet.

The Social Security program has been very popular up until now—the "third rail" of American politics. But how popular will the system continue to be when it pays much less than before on the contributions of the average American, much less than the bond rate? In addition to solving the previously mentioned actuarial balance problem, it would seem important to solve the rate-of-return problem to insure that in the future Social Security would give a better return on the contributions of most American workers.

Entitlement Spending

Social Security should not be looked at in isolation. To see if future benefits are affordable and at what tax rate, we must also take into consideration future levels of real wages and incomes. One side of this issue brings up the national saving question. As I argue in the next chapter, desirable Social Security reform packages should raise national saving to try to insure that the whole economy has the capacity to pay future benefits.

A related consideration involves overall entitlement spending. The aging of the baby boom population cohort, along with the rising relative cost of medical care, means that certain types of spending are rising rapidly in the United States. The general label for this rapidly rising spending is entitlement spending—spending for which beneficiaries are legally entitled, such as Social Security (the biggest component), Medicare (the most rapidly growing component), Medicaid, veteran's benefits, civil-service pensions, and some other programs. Rapid growth in entitlement spending can lay a claim on the nation's future output that is every bit as binding as sluggish growth in this output.

In this regard, the recent report of the Bipartisan Commission on Entitlements points to a serious problem, evident in figure 3.7. The figure shows different types of spending, and revenues, as a percentage of GDP. On the revenue side, for almost three decades now federal taxpayers have been willing to tax themselves between 19 and 20 percent of GDP, shown on the graph as the dashed line. Back in 1970 entitlement spending and interest payments together

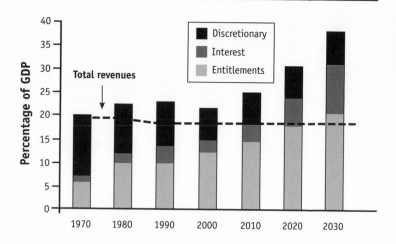

FIGURE 3.7. Federal outlays and revenues under present law. (From Bipartisan Commission on Entitlements and Tax Reform 1994, 7.)

accounted for only 7 percent of GDP, leaving a substantial marginal for other types of appropriated spending (for roads, schools, defense, research, and so forth). The share of GDP devoted to entitlement spending and interest then rose to 12 percent in 1980, 14 percent in 1990, and should come in at about 15 percent in 2000. Soon after this the baby boomers begin retiring, and the sum of entitlement spending and interest payments engulfs the entire federal budget (apart from deficit spending), at least until federal tax rates are raised. Every year more and more federal tax revenues are eaten up by entitlement spending, and if the country is to have anything left over to deal with the whole range of public priorities and programs, it will have to either limit the growth of entitlement spending or raise deficits or taxes. The lesson is similar to that shown in figure 3.4, except that the numbers are much more dramatic because they now include the dramatic rises in spending for the major health care programs. This prospective entitlement-spending growth heightens the nation's, and Social Security's, long-term financial concerns.

Policies

These issues set the stage for new policy changes. Somehow or other the country must bring the OASDI trust funds back into over-all financial balance. Somehow or other it makes sense to raise the rate of return, or money's worth, on the retirement contributions of younger people. Somehow or other the nation must raise its overall saving rate and/or limit the growth in entitlement spend-ing. How to do all these good things at once? Some ideas are given in the next chapters.

4

The Goals of Reform

It seems clear that some new approaches are in order for Social Security. The dominant policy response of the twentieth century, raising payroll taxes to pay for a fixed benefit schedule, could provide financing for the trust funds, but it locks Americans into steadily lower rates of return on increasingly large payroll contributions. Cutting benefits limits the payroll contributions but still lowers rates of return.

To deal with all dimensions of the problem requires some new approaches. In the next chapter I analyze a number of these new approaches. Here I set the stage for that discussion by proposing four goals of reform—to preserve the social protections of Social Security, to restore balance in the trust funds, to make Social Security more affordable economically, and to raise rates of return. Each of these goals will be explained and rationalized.[1]

Social Protections

Social Security's social protections have been in place for so long now it is easy to take them for granted. The high replacement rates for low-wage workers give these workers and their families protection against destitution in retirement years and move millions of aged individuals out of poverty status. The disability program gives disabled workers and their families protection against the financial consequences of severe workplace disabilities. There is early survivor's insurance for the family members of workers who die prematurely. Social Security benefits are also real annuities, which means that they continue as long as workers live, with added protection for surviving spouses. Not only that, but the automatic inflation adjustment means that these benefits automatically retain their real value as consumer prices rise, at this point one of the few pension programs in the United States that offers this protection.

In line with the new demographic and economic realities, it may be necessary to prune the future growth of Social Security benefits. But there is still broad agreement that whatever pruning takes place should not cut into these important social protections. There will obviously need to be judgments made about whether any pruning in the growth of benefits hurts the social protections, but there should be little controversy that preserving these protections is an important social goal.

Trust Fund Solvency

Using the traditional 75-year standard, the OASDI trust funds are now out of actuarial balance by 2.2 percent of covered payroll. Using the stronger and presumably more appropriate standard that the system should not become unbalanced because of the sheer passage of time, the deficit is closer to 3.3 percent of covered payroll. These deficits should be closed as soon as possible, by either tax or benefit changes.

Since the financial assets of the OASDI trust funds are not

likely to be exhausted until about 2029, it is easy to rationalize waiting to make changes. But waiting is a very bad idea, perhaps the worst suggestion anybody can make about Social Security. It should first be recognized that it is both politically difficult, and in a sense a violation of an implicit social contract, to cut benefits for current retirees. These people have worked throughout their careers trusting in a certain set of rules, and it would be unfair to change the rules once these workers have retired from their jobs and have much less chance of protecting themselves. It could also be destructive, if future retirees begin trusting less in the government's implicit promises.

If current retirees are to be largely protected from benefit cuts, which seems a sensible guideline, and if there are to be cuts in benefits, these cuts must begin very soon. To avoid serious equity issues between retirees of different ages, the cuts should be phased in gradually, and they should be in place soon enough that the baby boomers can be warned of their impact and make necessary revisions in their retirement plans. The enormous baby boom cohort will begin retiring in year 2008, and many of its members are making retirement plans right now. Leaving some time for congressional debate and action, for the cuts to be phased in, and for the baby boomers to revise their retirement plans, the time to begin changing the system is now.

Economic Affordability

There is an added dimension to the affordability problem. Not only must the long-term solvency of the OASDI trust funds be insured, but the *nation* must be able to afford the expected future Social Security program. The huge rise in numbers of aged individuals is more than a cost to the OASDI trust funds, it is a cost to the whole nation.

There are several dimensions to this affordability problem. One involves labor supply. Given the declining numbers of workers per beneficiary shown earlier in figure 3.3, costs would be more easily affordable if workers worked more, either through rising participation, longer hours, or by deferring retirement. Partly worker decisions about participation, hours, and retirement dates involve basic tastes—here, absent other considerations, government policy should strive to distort these decisions as little as possible. But partly these decisions are affected by government policy. To the extent that workers do not eventually get back the proceeds of their payroll taxes, the payroll tax to finance Social Security introduces what is known as a distortionary tax wedge, which many economists consider to lead to significant reductions in labor supply and to be one of the most significant costs of Social Security.[2] To the extent that retirement rules such as the earnings test reduce labor supply, there is again a potential loss of work effort.[3]

While there are continuing empirical debates on the size of these effects, the general policy strategies seem clear. As for payroll taxes, from a distortionary standpoint alone, the lower the better. Other things equal, a small-sized Social Security system with lower payroll taxes leads to fewer distortions and a bigger labor force than a large-sized Social Security system. As for the earnings test, early retirement possibilities, and the delayed retirement credit, the more neutral the better. These tests should be set so that workers do not gain or lose on average from retiring early or late, and the earnings test should be set to minimize work disincentives.

There is also a significant long-term dimension to the question of economic affordability. Most fundamental here is what is known as the national-saving issue. Were America to save more of its annual output, capital investment would rise, future output levels would rise, and future benefit levels would be more easily affordable. As was argued earlier, national saving could be raised by any measures to prefund future benefits, either through payroll tax increases in advance of benefit growth, or by measures to mandate or induce added pension saving.[4]

The prospective rapid growth of entitlement spending also enters in here. Figure 3.7 showed that under present trends it is only a matter of time before Social Security, Medicare, and Medicaid use up all federal revenues. Surely the nation does not want to get into a position where it cannot afford to spend on anything other than programs supporting the welfare of older people.

One way to avoid this situation is to limit the growth of entitlement spending. There are different types of entitlement spending, and in principle any could be limited. But in contrast to rationing medical care or limiting normal medical-reimbursement payments, a rationale for making at least some cuts in the future growth of Social Security benefits is that these changes only involve money. They do not involve more complicated and delicate matters such as rationing health care, limiting payments to health care providers, or endangering medical education or technology. As such, limiting the future growth of Social Security benefits may be one of the least costly and least complicated ways to cut the future growth of entitlement spending. Certainly high-income individuals would have many ways of protecting themselves, if the changes were made gradually and announced well in advance.

Rate of Return

Table 3.1 and figure 3.6 display Social Security in a new, and perhaps unfamiliar, light. In different ways they show the rate of return workers born at different dates receive on their overall payroll contributions. Over time, because of the maturing of the system and demographic and economic trends, this rate of return is diminishing. Whereas the typical present-day retiree has received more in the present value of benefit than he or she paid in payroll contributions, the typical younger worker is slated to receive significantly less.

Intergenerational equity is a tricky matter, and it would be inappropriate to conclude from this calculation alone that Social Security is unfair to younger workers. As mentioned earlier, some intergenerational transfers are almost inevitable when a significant defined-benefit program such as Social Security is first starting up. Moreover, older workers may have fought in World War II (or at least more of them fought in World War II than the younger workers who fought in Vietnam), and may on balance be owed something by the nation. Living standards are growing all the time, and older workers will, again on balance, be poorer than younger workers, though certainly not in every case. Developing reasonable standards of intergenerational equity in the presence of all these factors is next to impossible.

At the same time, in narrow political terms if the Social Security system is there, paying benefits to younger workers that are clearly less than the returns that would be paid by government bonds, and less relative to contributions than for older workers, the system's political popularity is bound to be threatened. For this reason alone, apart from the deeper equity issues, it makes sense to try to construct a system where the ratio of benefits to contributions is not automatically declining for younger and younger workers. In this sense it seems reasonable to try to put Social Security on a different financial footing.

Evaluation

To evaluate any set of Social Security reforms, a set of criteria is needed. I have suggested four—to preserve present-day social protections, to restore actuarial solvency to OASDI, to make the program affordable to the nation as a whole, and to raise the rate of return on worker contributions in the long run. Past discussions of Social Security reform have generally focused on just the first two criteria, but given the changing economic and political landscape, it seems important to add the latter two.

It is relatively easy to come up with reforms that satisfy one or two of the criteria listed above. The trick is to find reform packages that satisfy all four of the criteria. In the next chapter we see that only a small number of reforms meet this four-way test.

5

New Approaches

In early 1997 President Clinton's advisory council issued a report that suggested some new approaches to reforming Social Security.[1] While the council was strongly divided on some ultimate policy questions, it was more or less agreed on the goals of reform. All council members wanted to preserve the basic protections of Social Security, all wanted to preserve the finances of the OASDI trust funds, all wanted to raise the money's-worth ratios for younger workers and future workers, most wanted to raise overall national saving, and most wanted to stem the growth of entitlement spending. But council members suggested very different ways to achieve these goals, which led to their divisions.

In this chapter I consider prototype approaches of the sort the council proposed. These approaches generally reflect the types of Social Security reforms that are being considered around the world today. I begin by discussing some of the remedies that are commonly suggested and how they fall short, in terms of the criteria listed in the previous chapter, and then I consider the new approaches and how most of them fall short, again in terms of the criteria listed earlier. This all leads up to my own preferred proposal, the one that satisfies all four goals of reform.

Payroll Tax Increases

The standard past method for reforming Social Security has been to raise the payroll tax as needed to finance benefits. If this payroll tax increase were immediate, it would be about 3.3 percent of covered payroll, making for an overall OASDI rate of 15.7 percent, 7.85 percent on employers and 7.85 percent on employees. If there are delays, we can see what will happen from figures 3.4 and 3.5. No payroll tax increase would be strictly necessary until 2029, at which time the payroll tax would need to rise fairly rapidly to about 18 percent, 9 percent apiece on employers and employees. And then the tax would rise on up indefinitely, though at a slower rate of increase.

The dominant past approach for solving Social Security's financial problems has been to raise the payroll tax as needed to finance a given benefit schedule. This approach maintains social protections and finances the trust funds. But since it does not raise payroll taxes until benefits rise, there is no prefunding, no increase in national saving, and no provision for the long-term economic affordability of benefits. This approach also worsens the distortions due to Social Security and probably lowers the supply of labor. Since younger workers must pay more to receive the same benefits, it clearly worsens the rate of return realized by these younger workers.

A variant of this suggestion is to raise the taxable maximum ceiling, now $65,400. This change would raise payroll tax revenues by about 15 percent in the short run, but by much less in the long run because these newly paying high-wage workers would be entitled to benefits down the road. It would increase the economic distortions at the top of the wage scale, and it would drive down rates of return for high-wage earners even more than a general payroll tax increase.[2]

The approach of raising payroll taxes as needed to finance a given benefit schedule may have looked attractive in the twentieth century when Social Security was not a fully developed program and when there was rapid population and economic growth. But since none of those conditions are likely to obtain in the twenty-first century, the payroll tax approach is likely to become increasingly unattractive.

Benefit Cuts

An alternative approach is, of course, benefit cuts. Of the myriad ways to cut benefits, I discuss four—altering the price indexation procedure, means-testing benefits, changing the normal retirement age, and changing the benefit formula.

The CPI

One common suggestion for cutting benefits is to reduce the indexation of Social Security benefits for inflation, a suggestion made in the recent report of the commission studying the CPI.[3] The commission estimated there to be an upward bias in the consumer price index of about 1.1 percentage points a year. Were the indexation formula immediately adjusted downward by this amount, roughly half of the present long-term actuarial deficit could be eliminated.

Everybody seems to agree that there should be more or less complete inflation protection for retirees—that is, that benefits should be adjusted to keep up with the growth of prices. This is one of the fundamental advantages of Social Security right now. Everybody also agrees that the inflation protection should be accurate—that is, that there should not be payments to retirees beyond those necessary to keep up with the growth of prices. But beyond these near platitudes, the inflation protection issue becomes quite tricky.

To the extent that the Bureau of Labor Statistics (BLS) reviews the suggestions of outside committees and other outside experts and makes the requisite changes in its computation of the CPI, there is no particular controversy. Social Security benefits are already inflation-adjusted according to the BLS calculation, and the latter would simply be changed. While the BLS has already, or is in the process of, implementing some of the suggestions of the CPI commission, these changes alone will make only a modest saving for the OASDI trust funds. More thoroughgoing changes would require more speculative assumptions about quality improvements from new goods, speculative assumptions that official government statistical agencies are normally unwilling to make.

Some of those arguing for a stronger adjustment suggest that there be a separate calculation, or separate group, that determines inflation adjustments apart from the BLS. While such an approach is enticing, there are serious dangers. Before 1972, when real Social Security benefits and payroll tax rates were rising sharply, that was close to the situation. Decisions on how to index benefits for inflation were left to politicians, and not surprisingly in the end they reflected the wishes of those with the most to gain or lose, Social Security beneficiaries themselves. Not surprisingly, the end result was that Social Security benefits generally rose by more than would have been dictated by price increases alone. Twenty-five years ago it was viewed as both a political triumph and a money-saving measure to take indexation out of politics and to leave the inflation adjustments to the impartial BLS. Those who would want to reverse this process now may in the end cost the system money.

Means Testing

Another approach to cutting Social Security benefits, suggested by the Concord Coalition, is known as means testing. The idea is to reduce the normal benefits of high-income retirees by some fraction of the other income they have in retirement.

Again, there is wide agreement on the wisdom of a benefit schedule of the sort shown back in table 2.1, which gives much higher replacement rates to low-wage workers. It is also appropriate to apply normal income tax treatment to Social Security benefits, which has the effect of taxing these benefits at the normal progressive rates of the federal personal income tax. But the means testers are suggesting more. They urge that benefits for high-income retirees be reduced even more than would be implied by these standards. They would simply take away from 10 to 80 percent of the benefits received by high-income aged individuals.[4]

This approach may seem attractive politically. But unlike changes in the standard benefit schedule and the standard income tax treatment, means-testing singles out for especially harsh treatment those who have other income in retirement years—basically those who work while retired or those who have done private pension saving on top of Social Security. However Social Security develops, the nation will want to encourage people to work longer and to save more. What sense does it then make to penalize those who have engaged in these desirable behaviors? While there may be ways the underlying benefits of high-income workers can be pruned, means testing as such seems a violation of the long-term implicit promise of Social Security, in a way that discourages, rather than encourages, socially worthwhile behavior.[5]

The Normal Retirement Age

Another approach might be to alter the normal retirement age, now 65 but already legislated to rise to 67 gradually in the next century. Suppose it rose to 67 early in the next century and then kept on slowly climbing, at the same rate as overall life expectancy for adults. This would mean that all present workers would get benefits closer to the retirement protection envisioned in the original structure of Social Security, and that all future workers would spend about the same percentage of their adult lifetime paying for and collecting Social Security benefits. Since these future workers would be living longer into their retirement years, it is not unreasonable to make them pay into the trust funds more years.

Changes in the retirement age seem a reasonably fair way to limit Social Security costs and may be a part of a desirable reform package, but there are problems with overreliance on this one form of cutting benefits. While many workers arrive at age 65 good health and are physically able to work a few more years, not all are. There are still coal miners and other workers in physically demanding jobs, for whom the lengthened work careers could be a real imposition. Moreover, changes in the retirement age impose especial burdens on those with shorter life expectancies.

Changes in the Benefit Schedule

A final way to cut benefits is simply to change the benefit schedule, given back in figure 2.1. Suppose the replacement rates for high-income individuals were gradually lowered from their present level of 29 percent down to 25 or even 20 percent. What is the social cost of that? In the long run high-income wage earners would be getting about $12,000 per year, rather than a bit over $17,000. But there are other ways for them to buttress their benefits, particularly if the benefit cuts were phased in very gradually over time. These high-wage workers could relatively easily save more or work longer.

The implicit financial returns for high-income workers would gradually drop, but again there are other ways to raise that implicit rate of return. None of the key social protections of the living standards of low-wage workers would be disturbed by this pruning at the high end, nor would the protections against the financial consequences of disability, death, or inflation. There would be small changes in overall incentives to work and save, some in a positive direction, some in a negative direction. If it were desired to cut the growth of Social Security benefits, this would seem a very reasonable approach.

So there are wise and unwise ways of cutting benefits. If done in sensible ways, such as by incorporating any BLS changes into the indexation formula, slowly increasing the normal retirement age, and by a slight tilting of the benefit schedule, benefit cuts can preserve the underlying social protections of Social Security, and they would certainly improve the long-term solvency of the OASDI trust funds. They would not directly raise national saving much, but they would limit the growth in entitlement spending and do something to help make future Social Security benefits economically affordable. The only goal benefit cuts would not help promote is the rate-of-return goal: since they maintain contributions but lower benefits for some workers, these workers would get a lower return on their contributions.

New Approaches

The 1997 advisory council recommended three new approaches for dealing with Social Security. In this section I do not review the specifics of these plans, which can get very detailed. I analyze the broad, generic approaches suggested by the advisory council.

Defined Benefits Only

Social Security is a DB plan, largely on a PAYG basis. As long as it remains on a PAYG basis, it is impossible to achieve simultaneously all four goals proposed above. But if there were to be more pre-funding of future benefits, it would be possible to achieve all four goals.

The most straightforward way to do this is to raise the payroll tax a small amount, say 2 percentage points, have the money go to the OASDI trust funds, but then let the trust funds invest in pools of common stock, instead of government bonds as now.[6] The pay-roll tax increase would represent a cut in current consumption, or new national saving, to help make benefits economically afford-able in the long run. If returns on common stocks continue to out-pace returns on bonds, as they have in the past,[7] the long-term solvency of the OASDI trust funds could be restored. The same con-dition would raise rates of return realized by younger workers.

A group of advisory council members suggested a similar approach, called the Maintain Benefits (MB) plan.[8] The impact of this plan on future money's-worth ratios, under the standard assumptions of the advisory council, is shown in figure 5.1 (the same as fig. 3.6). The approach eventually stabilizes money's-worth ratios at between 90 and 100 percent, satisfying this inter-generational political criterion. But this group made a key change in the plan because it did not favor an early rise in the payroll tax, hence eliminating the main economic rationale for such a plan. Without a payroll tax increase, there would be no change in national saving, no prefunding of benefits, and no provision to make future benefits economically affordable. While such a change

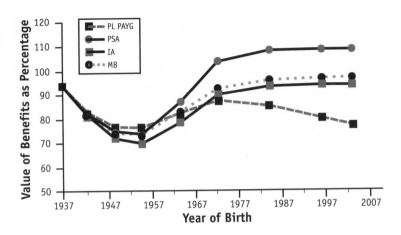

FIGURE 5.1. Present value of expected OASDI benefits as a percentage of present value of expected contributions, for composite workers, by year of birth. (From Advisory Council on Social Security 1997.)

might make the MB plan more salable politically, it becomes less attractive economically.

There are other problems. In these types of plans it should be noted that the OASDI trust funds would be holding sizable amounts of common stock—about $1 trillion at today's levels in the MB plan, one-seventh of all U.S. holdings of common stock. Since Social Security is now included in the federal budget, this would be the first time budget funds were actually used to buy common stock. One could raise a number of questions about how such a change might work. Would it increase the intrusiveness of government regulation of business? How would the government's shares be voted? Would it impede the ability of the Congress to arrive at budgetary agreements (since there would now be the precedent of borrowing more to finance stock purchases)? Some of these issues could be dealt with by having Social Security removed from the federal budget, but so far even that has proven impossible to accomplish.[9]

These issues are important and could be further studied—indeed, at the eleventh hour even the MB contingent of the advisory council watered down its proposal to that of a proposition that should be studied. But it takes little study to recognize that a key problem here is the lack of prefunding. Whether Social Security remains a DB system or has some DC elements, whether the rise is in payroll taxes or in private-pension contributions, there should be some increases in national saving. Without this new saving, no Social Security proposal looks very attractive.

Defined Contribution Mainly

An alternative approach to dealing with Social Security that is getting attention these days, in this country and abroad, is to change the present DB system to a large-scale defined-contribution (DC) plan. While the term *privatization* of Social Security can be very vague, schemes of this sort would generally give workers more control over their own retirement funds and hence qualify as privatization schemes. The details could vary, but generally these plans would let younger workers invest their payroll taxes on their own. Older workers would usually be kept on the present system, leading to some significant transition costs. Also, there are a series of questions about how much control workers should be allowed to exercise over their DC accounts.

One version of such an approach was suggested by another group of advisory council members, called the Personal Security Accounts (PSA) plan.[10] This plan would keep workers age 55 and over on the present system and put all workers under age 25 on an entirely new system, with those between 25 and 54 on a hybrid system. Instead of paying a payroll tax of 12.4 percent to OASDI, younger workers would pay only 7.4 percent to OASDI, an amount that would finance a flat benefit that starts at about $5,000 a year (wage indexed over time), survivor's and disability insurance, and some transition expenses. These workers would be required to invest the remaining 5 percent of their covered earnings in individual accounts, called Personal Security Accounts. Using the empirical finding that about half the funds in existing accounts with similar features are invested in common stocks, and again assuming that stocks continue to outperform bonds, the PSA plan stabilizes future money's-worth ratios at more than 100 percent (fig. 5.1).

An important drawback of the PSA plan is that of transition costs. Since older workers would be kept on the present system and younger workers would have a large share of their taxes going into accounts for their own retirement, there is a generational hole in the financing of public-retirement costs. Middle-aged workers have spent much of their careers paying payroll taxes to retirees and do not have much time left in their careers to accumulate for their own retirement. As the next chapter will show, when systems such as the PSA plan have been adopted in other countries, these middle-aged workers have simply been given the benefit credits they have built up under the previous system and then asked to save for their own retirement from then on. Redeeming these benefit credits will generate huge transition costs. In the PSA plan, for example, the transition cost amounts to an added 1.5 percent of payroll for more than 70 years. It is high in the beginning, leading to a large amount of new governmental borrowing, and then tapers off in the twenty-first century as these middle-age workers gradually die off. While in many ways plans like the PSA plan seem deceptively attractive, these transition costs must be kept firmly in mind—there will need to be some combination of significant new tax increases and significant new government borrowing in any PSA-type plan. Advocates rejoin that the implicit liabilities are there anyway, and these transition expenses merely form a recognition of these liabilities, but in the present political climate new tax increases and new borrowing could still be quite unpopular.

A second problem with a PSA plan involves its riskiness, really the fact that it transfers much financial risk from the government to individuals, in three separate ways.

First, Social Security benefits would be cut significantly, all the way from the levels given in table 2.1 down to the flat benefit that will be below the poverty line for some time. If people's investments do badly, there will not be much left for these folks to fall back on.

The second way involves the management of the accounts. When people are told to take some share of their payroll tax and invest it on their own, a huge number of issues could be raised. Where can people hold these assets, in recognized financial institutions or in their mattresses? How are the accounts to be regulated to insure investment safety? How can these accounts be effectively regulated, in a country with 140 million potential holders of these PSA accounts, many of them very small? Would not financial institutions charge large administrative fees to manage these smaller accounts? What would happen if many investments were to go bad and many people forced to live in retirement on their relatively meager flat benefit?

A final potential difficulty involves the distribution of the accounts. On retirement, should the accumulated funds be mandatorily converted to real annuities, to give people protection against outliving their assets, and against inflation, or would people be able to decide how to spend down their accumulations on their own? If people cannot be trusted to save enough in their working years (remember, the PSA plan requires people to hold DC accounts of a certain size), should they be trusted to keep enough assets in their accounts once they reach retirement age? They still may have forty years to live.[11]

Answers to these questions could range all over the map. The advisory council group recommending the PSA plan took a rather minimalist stance on many of these regulatory issues—the accounts would have to be in certified financial institutions but with very little further regulatory restrictions and no requirements to annuitize. This strong free-market stance would appear to introduce a great deal of unnecessary risk into the retirement-saving issue—risk that people would not invest their funds safely and risk that young retirees might overconsume their assets. Changes could be made that would lessen these risks, but there would still be greater risk than in the other approaches.

In terms of our four goals, the flat benefit and the continued disability and survivor's protection would continue at least a small-scale DB component of the PSA plan, but some of the present social protections for middle-income workers would clearly be lost. The plan would restore the solvency of the OASDI trust funds, but these trust funds would have a much diminished role in supporting overall retirement saving. Even with the transition tax, more workers' payroll contributions would fund their own retirement, leading to a probable increase in labor supply. The transition tax would represent new national saving, and the benefit cut would limit entitlement-spending growth, so the PSA plan scores well on grounds of economic affordability. It also scores well on rate-of-return grounds (see fig. 5.1), though for this plan particularly there should be more careful examination of the variance of these rates of return.[12]

A Mixed Plan

There must be something between a simple continuation of the present DB system and a dramatic and wholesale switch to large-scale reliance on DC accounts. Cannot some of the rate-of-return advantages of the PSA plan be sacrificed to achieve greater safety, and to avoid the difficult transition costs?

In fact, there is something. Another group on the advisory council suggested a middle way, as did Senators Robert Kerrey and Alan Simpson as a result of work on the Entitlements Commission, and as did the Committee for Economic Development.[13]

As with the other approaches, there could be many variants of this middle way. One that has received much attention is the individual-accounts (IA) plan of the advisory council, given in full in the appendix. In this plan there are two central components.

- A gradual phased-in cut in the future growth of benefits for high-wage workers, enough to constrain the future growth of pension spending and to bring the OASDI trust funds back to solvency with indefinite continuation of the present 12.4 percent payroll tax rate.

- New mandatory DC accounts, called Individual Accounts, on top of Social Security. These accounts would represent the vital new national saving, raising future GDP and making the plan economically affordable.[14] They would be privately owned but publicly managed, hence simplifying administration and reducing riskiness. If it matters, the public management of the individual accounts means that such a plan probably would not be considered a true privatization of Social Security.

The public management of the individual accounts simplifies administration and reduces the risk that the accounts will be misinvested. The SSA could collect the money and allocate it according to investor choices, into a menu of from five to ten broad market index funds, covering stocks and bonds alike. The funds would give investors average market returns, but with less risk than is implicit in the holding of individual stocks or bonds.[15] The funds would also be annuitized on retirement, to eliminate the risk that people will overspend in their early retirement years.

The benefit cuts, accomplished as described above through a combination of changes in BLS indexing, the normal retirement age and the benefit schedule, would restore the long-term solvency of the OASDI trust funds and limit the future growth of entitlement spending—the ratio of Social Security spending to GDP would be held approximately constant into the twenty-first century under such a plan. Since these cuts would focus on high-wage, nondisabled workers, they could be accomplished with minimal damage to the key social protections of Social Security. Since the cuts would phase in gradually and in any case would only be cuts in the growth of benefits, there would be no benefit cuts for current-day retirees. There would also be no change in payroll tax rates and in economic distortions.

The combination of benefit cuts and the new individual accounts leads to rates of return, or money's-worth ratios, not quite as high as in the other plans (fig. 5.1), but the long-term money's-worth ratios still stabilize between 90 and 100 percent, hence satisfying this political criterion. Beyond that, of all the plans suggested by the advisory council, the IA plan is the only plan that fulfills all four goals of Social Security reform.

There are some other ways to look at the IA plan. One is that it requires sacrifice on all margins. There are some cuts in benefits, some rises in the retirement age, some required new saving, and some use of new stock market investment opportunities. Given that there are reasons for changing Social Security, it makes economic sense to change a bit in each of these ways, as opposed to relying entirely on one single change. This even-handed approach prevents a situation in which particular individuals take particularly big losses.

The IA plan is also the most straightforward economically. The

MB plan has stock market investment not backed up by new saving. Where do the new stock market funds come from? There must be a great amount of asset shuffling, with the OASDI funds holding more stocks and fewer bonds and the private sector holding more bonds and fewer stocks. Total assets held by the nation, and total national wealth, would be unchanged. To view this switch from another perspective, the greater returns people realize on their Social Security accounts would then be offset by the lower returns people would realize on their own portfolios (which would have fewer stocks and more bonds). Rates of returns on stocks and bonds might also be changed by this forced asset swap—there would likely be rises in real interest rates and drops in stock returns.

The PSA plan has people holding their new DC accounts, but to a large degree financed by the large-scale transition borrowing. The government would in effect be borrowing at low bond rates to finance plan benefits, permitting people to invest at higher stock market rates. This process is known as arbitrage in financial circles. This arbitrage cuts into the attractiveness, and the new wealth creation, of the PSA plan.

The IA plan, by contrast, has no asset swaps and no arbitrage. The OASDI trust funds would be brought into balance and people would be required to make new saving, presumably investing the funds in the way they invested their old saving. The changes are straightforward, the new saving is clear, and there would be minimal disruption of normal asset markets and prices.

Finally, the IA plan gives more balance in the nation's pension system than the other plans. The DB-only plans with stock market investment do not have major investment risk because stock market investments will be done centrally, but they contain all the DB risks of the present system—if economic growth or the number of new workers falls short, benefits must be reduced. The plans with large-scale reliance on DC accounts contain a great deal of investment risk. The mixed IA plan contains a small amount of DB risk and a small amount of DC risk and therefore may be preferred from a risk minimization standpoint.

Politics

A final test is political—will such a plan pass? There are again possibilities and risks.

First, as for the third-rail analogy, none of these advisory council plans cut the benefits of current retirees. Those plans with benefit cuts, the PSA plan and the IA plan, make them in the future, with plenty of time for younger workers to revise their saving and retirement plans. Generally these younger workers are better off in both plans. Hence the political calculus would seem favorable, with present retirees no worse off and younger workers better off.

The IA plan brings Social Security into financial balance, with some benefit cuts and some required pension contributions. But there are none of the features that seem likely to prove unpopular politically—no cuts in benefits for present retirees, no tax increases, no transition borrowing, no large-scale purchases of common stocks with budget funds. Beyond that, the IA plan has a sensible mixture of retained social protection with new responsibilities for individuals to provide some funds for their own retirement.

There are, of course, some political risks. One is that the mandatory individual accounts will prove unpopular. If so, it would always be possible to try to induce people to save voluntarily on top of Social Security, carefully warning them of their reduced future benefits in case they do not save. Or, it would be possible to cut benefits by more and carve the individual accounts out of the present 12.4 percent payroll contribution, as is done in the Kerrey-Simpson plan.

An opposite risk is that the individual accounts will prove too popular, making the OASDI system suffer in comparison. In any system that combines relatively high-yielding DC components with relatively low-yielding DB components, there may be pressure to divert funds to the DC components, hence reducing the redistribution within Social Security. It is hard to know how to evaluate this latter risk against the alternative, which is to let the OASDI system just raise taxes and pay progressively lower rates of return, suffering growing political unpopularity on its own accord.

Assessment

Now that the demographics and economics of the nation have changed, it seems indispensable to begin thinking about new approaches to Social Security. With standard approaches of tax increases and/or benefit cuts, it is possible to preserve social protections and to bring the OASDI system into financial balance. But it may not be possible to make plans economically affordable, and it certainly is not possible to raise their rate of financial return. Surely the nation wants a retirement system it can afford, one that gives decent value to cohorts of younger workers.

There are still various ways of accomplishing all four goals mentioned throughout this book, but many plans that might have made sense in a two-goal world no longer look so attractive. One that looks very attractive even in the four-goal world is to retain the essence of the present benefit system, pruned back to limit future benefit growth, coupled with small-scale, prefunded DC accounts. This is the only approach that both preserves the important social protections of Social Security and also raises national saving. In the end such a system may remain truest to the original vision of Social Security, modernized to take account of the demographics and economics of the twenty-first century.

6

Looking Outward

For a developed country the United States is a relative latecomer to the social-security business. By the time the United States adopted its system in 1935, 11 European countries already had systems, with Germany's being nearly 50 years old! Even though OASDI spending in the United States was $347 billion in fiscal 1995, that amounted to less than 5 percent of U.S. GDP, a relatively low ratio by world standards. According to the World Bank, the U.S. ratio of public pension spending to GDP is only 70 percent of the average for Organization of Economic Cooperation and Development (OECD) countries, less than half the share in countries such as Italy and Austria.

Looking ahead, the United States system also seems to be in relatively good financial shape. Seventy-five-year forecasts for the OASDI trust funds do indicate a sizable deficit, but these financial problems are again modest by world standards. Populations are aging and pension costs are rising around the world, generally more rapidly than in the United States. Existing pension systems are usually more generous than that of the United States, at least in the developed world. The United States is looking at a younger population and lower future pension liabilities (compared to its GDP) than almost all developed countries.

But the fact that present or future difficulties in financing pension spending may loom larger abroad than here could be cold comfort. They loom large enough here, certainly large enough that the experience of other countries is relevant and interesting. This chapter looks outward, to assess the magnitude of the challenges faced elsewhere and the differing responses in other parts of the world. I focus particularly on challenges and changes taking place in Europe, Australia, and Latin America. Perhaps the United States can learn, either from the problems facing other countries or from their responses to the challenges. While the United States may have been a latecomer in adopting a social-security system in the twentieth century, perhaps it could be a leader in the twenty-first century.

Aging Populations, Rising Costs

Chapter 3 identified the magic 2.1 fertility rate. If women have on average more than 2.1 babies, populations expand and have a relatively high share of young people. If women have on average less than 2.1 babies, populations contract and have a relatively high share of old people. Around the world fertility rates are generally dropping, already to levels well below 2.1 in most developed countries and to levels approaching 2.1 in most developing countries. Combining this trend with the fact that in general people are living longer because of the welcome improvement in health standards, we can see why most countries in the world are now facing aging populations.

World Bank data on population aging are shown in figure 6.1. The 22 OECD countries, covering all of Western Europe, Canada, the United States, Australia, and Japan, had (on average) 18 percent of their population over age 60 in 1990, but this share is projected to rise to 31 percent by 2030. As the figure also shows, the share over

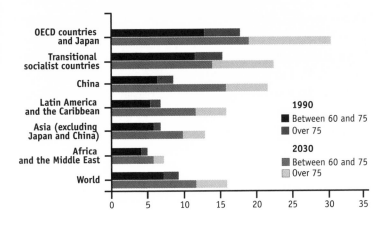

FIGURE 6.1. Percentage of population over 60 years old, by region, 1990 and 2030. (Adapted from World Bank 1994.)

age 75—individuals for whom the social cost of care is much higher—is expected to more than double over that same time span. This is roughly the pattern in the United States alone, though with the aging proportions at a somewhat lower level (all U.S. population ratios are about 90 percent of those shown in figure 6.1 for the OECD).

The share of aged people is generally less in the rest of the world, where fertility rates are generally higher and life expectancies are generally lower than in the OECD countries. But populations are still aging throughout this part of the world. The share of population over age 60 is expected to rise from 15 percent to 23 percent in the transitional socialist countries, from 8 to 22 percent in China, from 7 to 13 percent in the rest of Asia, from 7 to 16 percent in Latin America, and from 5 to 8 percent in Africa and the Middle East. In percentage terms, most of these increases are likely to outpace those of the OECD countries. Moreover, as with the

OECD, the share of individuals over age 75 is rising even more rapidly in each geographical area.

Just as is the case in this country, these higher aged population dependency ratios mean higher future social spending for older people. The most significant increases will be for health spending, but even apart from health spending, pension costs are slated to rise sharply. The World Bank's projected costs under present law for public pension spending (ignoring health costs) are shown in figure 6.2. For the OECD countries, the public pension spending ratio is expected to rise from 8 percent of GDP in 1990 to 17 percent in 2050 (the United States is now 80 percent of the OECD average but should be less than that in 2050). Public pension spending ratios for the other countries start off lower but grow more, and by 2050 all pension costs but those of Africa and the Middle East should be at 10 percent or more of GDP.

Hence, compared to the rest of the world, the United States is a relatively high-income country with a relatively sound present system, relatively low pension burdens, and a population that is aging at relatively slow rates. If there is felt to be a Social Security problem in this country, the challenges must be that much greater around the globe. How are these other countries meeting these challenges?

Differing Approaches

With so many countries facing so many different situations and having so many different institutions, it is hard to draw simple lessons. The World Bank has tried to develop a blueprint for reform, called a three-pillar system. The first pillar refers to a redistributive component, either a flat benefit or a minimum pension guarantee, financed either by general revenues or by a trust fund. The

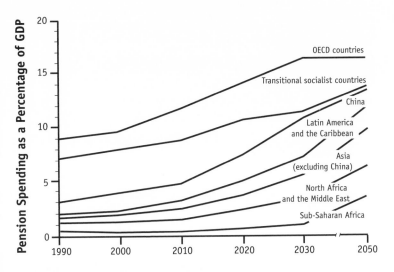

FIGURE 6.2. Projected public pension spending, by region, 1990–2050. This projection assumes that the current relationship between demography and spending continues. (From World Bank 1994.)

second pillar refers to DC-style mandatory individual accounts, and the third pillar to voluntary saving.[1] Since most developed countries have some sort of a flat benefit or a DB system with significant redistribution, and most have voluntary saving, the key issue raised by the bank is whether there should be a DC element, the bank's second pillar. In the U.S. context, both the PSA and the IA plans answer in the affirmative and the MB plan in the negative.

However this decision should be made in this country, the World Bank's blueprint permits categorization of pension reforms around the world. At this point relatively few OECD countries have even attempted to reform their costly DB systems, but some of those countries who have reformed have introduced DC components. Examples are the United Kingdom and Australia. And in Latin America, where existing DB systems leave more to be desired, there are the beginnings of a much more widespread shift to pre-funded DC systems.

Europe

The most established pension plans are in the European countries. Social Security details on 12 of the 15 countries in the European Union are shown in table 6.1. All countries have some combination of a flat benefit and an earned-right system, where workers who have contributed more payroll taxes get more benefits.

Populations are aging in each of these countries. The left two columns of the table show that the aged dependency ratio (the population of those 65 and over divided by the population aged 15–64) is projected to nearly double, rising from 21.4 percent in 1990 to 40

TABLE 6.1. Pension Data in European Countries

Country	Aged Dependency Ratio		Pension Expense/GDP		Pension Liability/G
	1990	2030	1995	2040	1995-2070
Belgium	22.4	41.1	10.4	15.0	153
Denmark	22.7	37.7	6.8	11.6	n.a.
Germany	21.7	49.2	11.1	18.4	62
Spain	19.8	41.0	10.0	16.8	109
France	20.8	39.1	10.6	14.3	102
Ireland	18.4	25.3	3.6	2.9	19
Italy	21.6	48.3	13.3	21.4	60
Netherlands	19.1	45.1	6.0	12.1	53
Portugal	19.5	33.5	7.1	15.2	109
Finland	19.7	41.1	10.1	18.0	65
Sweden	27.6	39.4	11.8	14.9	132
United Kingdom	24.0	38.7	4.5	5.0	24
Average	21.4	40.0	8.8	13.8	81

Source: Davis 1997.

percent in 2030. While having just average aged dependency ratios now, populations in Germany and Italy should age the most, with the aged dependency ratio there rising to nearly 50 percent.[2]

The next columns give even worse news for these countries. The third and fourth columns show projections of public pension costs relative to GDP for the 12 countries. In 1995 these pension costs averaged 8.8 percent of GDP. This is already much higher than the ratio in the United States (4.8 for Social Security alone, a bit more if some other smaller public pension programs are included) because the European systems typically feature higher replacement rates and earlier retirement ages. But this gap is expected to widen considerably in the next 50 years. While the baby boom retirement crunch would bring the U.S. ratio up to about 8 percent of GDP under present law, it would raise the European ratio to 13.8 percent of GDP, with again Germany and Italy in particularly dire shape.

The right column of the table summarizes this information by computing the aggregate public pension liability relative to GDP. In the United States this liability is now about $2.5 trillion, 34 percent of GDP.[3] In Europe it averages 81 percent of GDP and is over 100 percent of GDP in Belgium, Spain, France, Portugal, and Sweden. Clearly European public pension systems are looking at some very significant future liabilities. If these countries do not make changes, their entitlement spending and payroll tax distortions will rise sharply, and their national saving and rates of return will fall sharply.

Most of these countries have done relatively little about these looming public pension costs. One exception is the United Kingdom, which for the past decade has been engaged in an incremental process of pension reform. While the U.K. population ratios look very average in table 6.1, note that both their public pension spending and liabilities are strikingly below those in the rest of Europe (and below those in the United States).

The U.K. system starts with a basic flat benefit of about 15 percent of the average wage for all workers, financed on a PAYG basis. On top of this is a state earnings-related pension scheme (SERPS), first introduced in the mid-1970s but scaled back since that time. The distinctive feature of the U.K. system is that firms and workers are allowed to opt out of SERPS, much as in Senator Clark's proposed amendment to the U.S. Social Security system back in the 1930s. And many workers do opt out. About half the labor force is now in company-run pensions (either of the DB or DC form) and another quarter are in personal pensions of the DC form. Rate-of-return studies show that returns on these private pensions options have exceeded, and are likely to continue exceeding, the implicit return on the SERPS, only partly because there are some subsidies for the personal pensions.[4]

The U.K. approach shows one way to evolve toward a prefunded system. The fact that a large share of the workforce has opted out of the public SERPS system in favor of prefunded pensions cuts back the future public pension and tax burdens and raises rates of return and likely future national saving. On the cost side, there are added risks and administrative costs for the private pensions. Moreover, the fact that workers can switch voluntarily means that the implicit redistribution the overall system can make is greatly limited. As was argued earlier, permitting voluntary opting out could leave the public system with all those who benefit from redistribution. This greatly raises the cost of redistribution and threatens the political popularity of the system. From this standpoint it would seem preferable to have a mandatory system, with some prefunding but with all workers forced to participate in the system's redistribution.

Another European country contemplating a switch to a different type of system is that cradle of the welfare state, Sweden. There a 1994 committee report proposed some significant departures. The present Swedish system features a flat benefit with an earnings-related supplement, each costing on the order of 4 or 5 percent of GDP. The earnings supplement is of the DB type, with substantial internal redistribution. But there are some perhaps unintended side effects. Since benefits are computed on the basis of the top 15 years of earnings, the benefit formula gives an edge to those with short but high-income careers (such as university graduates) and takes away from those with long but low-income careers.

The 1994 committee suggested a movement to greater actuarial fairness through a device called notional individual accounts. These accounts would not be prefunded, but the returns would be computed as if they were, with a yield equal to the standard PAYG return of the rate of growth of economy. The notional individual accounts would then lessen the internal redistribution of the system. To the extent that this redistribution is an unintended result of the DB rules, there could be some gain; to the extent that the redistribution is intended to support low-wage workers in their retirement, there could be some loss (though the Swedish report never challenged the flat benefit, which brings about most of the Swedish redistribution). But as compared to real prefunded individual accounts, the Swedish notional individual accounts have what appears to be a significant disadvantage in that they do not raise national saving, they do nothing to make future pension costs economically affordable, and their rate of return will generally fall short of that on true individual accounts that are invested in stocks and bonds.[5]

Australia

Whether due to the tilt of the globe or some other imponderable factor, pension reform has proceeded more rapidly in the southern hemisphere. One example is Australia, which is evolving a system similar to the PSA plan described in the previous chapter. For nearly a century now Australia has had a general-revenue-financed flat benefit costing around 3 percent of GDP, subject to both an earnings test and an asset test. These tests mean that the supposed flat benefit is really not flat—it phases out for retirees with high earnings and/or high assets.

Since this means-tested flat benefit can exert a strong disincentive for workers to accumulate, and for other reasons, beginning in the 1990s employers have been required to provide pension benefits for all employees, called superannuation accounts. While some of the older superannuation accounts are DB, most of the newer ones are DC, with contribution rates that are gradually rising up to 9 percent of wages, to a maximum amount. These mandatory DC contributions are taxed in a way that is slightly more favorable than the standard income tax treatment. Hence by the next century Australia will have largely prefunded its pension costs through a mixed DB-DC system.[6]

The large-scale reliance on DC accounts raises all the issues brought up in chapter 5, though the Australian superannuation accounts are managed by firms and not by individual workers. But these superannuation accounts are not required to be annuitized on retirement and indeed can be spent down when workers reach the age of 55. For low-wage workers without much in their superannuation accounts, there is thus a huge incentive to spend down the accounts and then actually receive *more* from the means-tested flat benefit. Any increased saving during the working years is thus offset by a huge incentive to decumulate early in retirement years. The obvious solution would be to require either full or partial annuitization of the superannuation accounts, and to make the flat benefit truly flat, eliminating the disincentive to work and save. This latter point exactly parallels the difficulties pointed out earlier for means testing in this country.

Latin America

Even more radical changes are being made in Latin America. Leading the parade is Chile. Back in 1981 the government scrapped its old DB system—which had uneven benefits across industries, incomplete coverage, and was very underfinanced (none of these are problems with the current United States system). In its place was inserted a DC system, close to the PSA proposal discussed in the previous chapter.

The first pillar of the Chilean system consists of a minimum pension guarantee financed by general revenues. The second pillar consists of large-scale individual accounts, funded by a mandatory contribution of 10 percent of payrolls. These are individually owned, but they must be invested in accounts held by about 30 certified private financial institutions. No individual can hold accounts in more than one financial institution (called AFPs, Asso-ciacion de Fondos de Pension), though individuals are free to switch their accounts. The AFPs collect the contributions from employers, a relatively expensive way to collect the funds. The government guarantees that the return on the funds falls within a certain range of the average among all AFP accounts.

The Chilean system solved the transition problem by giving workers with accruals under the previous system recognition bonds, payable when the employees retire. These recognition bonds were, and are to be, financed out of the existing government surplus. At retirement, the funds can either be taken out as a lump sum or annuitized, but workers are required to have a certain minimum annuity.[7]

While it would takes years to do a realistic evaluation of such a significant pension reform, superficially the Chilean system appears to be working well. The AFP funds have grown rapidly and have made good returns—12 percent in real terms in the 1980s, though less in the 1990s. About 40 percent of the assets are held in government bonds, with the remainder spread between domestic stocks and international equities. Overall participation rates have risen from 50 percent of the workforce under the old system to 60 percent under the new system. Administrative costs are high, far above those in the U.S. Social Security system but comparable to those on other Chilean pension systems. National saving rates for Chile have risen significantly since the pension reform, but it is difficult to tell how much of the rise was due to pension reform and how much was due to other factors.[8]

Five other Latin American nations—Peru, Argentina, Colombia, Uruguay, and Mexico—have already implemented similar two-pillar structures, and more systems are on the drawing boards. Generally the first pillar pays either a flat benefit or a minimum guarantee financed by general revenues and the second pillar a private DC individual account financed by mandatory payroll contributions. Both the minimum benefits and the DC payroll contributions vary widely across the countries. Lump sum withdrawals at retirement time are often permitted, though usually workers must annuitize enough of their accounts to guarantee a minimum pension benefit. Unlike Chile, all of these countries but Mexico permit workers to choose for a second pillar either the DC plan or a newly reformed DB plan—an option that may raise the cost of redistribution if it sends most of those benefiting from redistribution to the DB system. Most of these countries limited their past benefit accruals for current workers by raising their normal retirement age. They also put in place a regulatory structure to restrict the types of investments made in the individual accounts.[9]

Assessment

Populations are aging around the world, pension costs are rising sharply, and rates of return are falling. Many countries are not responding to these looming challenges at all, and some are making only marginal changes in their DB systems, changes that would not satisfy all of our four criteria for successful reform given in the previous chapters.

But many countries—the United Kingdom, Australia, and Chile among them—are making much more radical changes in their systems. They are moving in the direction of what the World Bank calls a two-pillar system—a basic flat benefit with DC individual accounts on top of that. These new systems are not perfect, and each of them still has many flaws. At the same time, the new reform efforts do represent early signs that countries are struggling with ways to prefund their retirement costs looming on the horizon in the next century. Perhaps the United States can learn from the experience of these other countries, and perhaps still other countries can then learn from the United States.

Appendix

Publicly Held
Individual Accounts

One group of advisory council members favors an individual-accounts (IA) plan. The goal is to preserve the social-adequacy protections in the present Social Security benefit system while still raising overall national retirement saving. The social-adequacy protections are largely preserved, though the growth of Social Security benefits would be gradually reduced. Part of this reduction in the growth of benefits applies to workers at all earnings levels resulting from an acceleration in the increase in the age of eligibility for full retirement benefits up to year 2011, followed by a slower increase in line with overall longevity, and by lengthening the computation period from 35 to 38 years. Part of the reduction in growth is focused primarily on middle- and high-wage workers because it comes from an adjustment in the benefit schedule, though with some reductions in spouse's benefits and improvements in survivor's protection. There would be a mandatory additional contribution of 1.6 percent of covered payroll that would be held by the government as defined-contribution individual accounts. Individuals would have constrained investment choices on how these funds were to be invested—ranging from a portfolio consisting entirely of bond index funds to equity index funds. The accumulation from the individual accounts would be converted by the government to single or joint minimum-guarantee indexed annuities when individuals elect retirement, which could happen any time after the present age of earliest eligibility for Social Security retirement benefits (age 62). The combination of the reduced growth in benefits, the increased age of eligibility for full retirement benefits, and the proceeds of the individual accounts would leave total benefits on average at about the levels of present law for all income groups.

The important specific provisions are as follows:

Mandatory defined contribution individual accounts in the amount of 1.6 percent of covered payroll would be created.

Defined-contribution individual accounts in the amount of 1.6 percent of covered payroll would be created and funded by employee contributions. Individuals would have constrained choices on how the funds were to be invested. These individual accounts would be clearly excluded from the federal budget, though the budgetary treatment of the rest of Social Security would remain unchanged.

The accumulated funds would be converted to single or joint minimum-guarantee indexed annuities when the individual elects retirement, any time after the age of earliest eligibility for benefits (now age 62).[1] The minimum-guarantee provision would assure that some portion of the purchase price of the annuity—say, an amount equal to one year's worth of the annuity—would be payable in all cases. Thus, even if a worker who had elected a single annuity died after receiving only one annuity payment, an additional sum would be paid to the survivors. As is the case with other pension plans, a married worker would have a choice (with the consent of the spouse) on whether a single or "joint and survivor" annuity was chosen. (The "joint and survivor" option would provide a lower basic annuity while the worker was alive but would continue to pay a portion of the annuity to the survivor after the worker's death.)

The gradual increase in the age of eligibility for full retirement benefits would be accelerated and extended.

The increase in the age of eligibility for full retirement benefits from 65 to 67 would be accelerated. After year 2011, when this age of eligibility reaches 67, it would rise slowly along with overall longevity. At present rates, this age would rise about 1 month every 2 years, meaning that it would reach age 70 by year 2083.[2]

The growth of basic benefits would be slowed, mainly for middle- and high-wage workers.

The 32 and 15 percent conversion factors in the present benefit schedule would be gradually lowered over time to 22.4 and 10.5 percent, respectively. Benefit changes would be phased in to avoid notches, or drops in real benefit levels, while keeping the basic OASDI tax rate at 12.4 percent of taxable payroll. The combination of all changes in benefits and the individual accounts would on average keep full benefits (including the proceeds of the individual accounts) at roughly present levels for all income classes of workers.

Survivor's protection for two-earner couples would be increased, and dependent spouse benefits would be lowered.

A surviving spouse's benefit would be determined as the highest of (1) his or her own basic benefit, (2) the deceased spouse's basic benefit, or (3) 75 percent of the couple's combined basic benefits. This change would increase benefits for survivors of two-earner couples. The dependent-spouse benefit would be gradually phased down from 50 percent to 33 percent of the worker's benefit. If the worker died before becoming eligible for retirement benefits, the survivor would have to wait to receive 75 percent of the combined benefit until the deceased would have become eligible.

Regular Social Security benefits would be taxed under income tax principles and deposited in the OASDI trust funds.

All Social Security benefits in excess of already taxed employee contributions would be included in federal taxable income. The income thresholds would be gradually phased out. Both provisions are the same as those in the MB reform plan. But unlike that plan, there would be no redirection of taxes on Social Security benefits from the health insurance trust fund to the OASDI trust funds.

All state and local government employees hired after 1997 would be covered under Social Security.

The benefit computation period would be extended from 35 to 38 years, phased in over the 1997–99 period.

Proceeds from the defined-contribution individual accounts would be taxed under consumption tax principles.

The individual accounts would not be included in the federal budget. To conform their tax treatment with the tax treatment of other defined-contribution pension saving, the individual accounts could be taxed in either of two ways.

1. They could be made tax deductible when saved and taxable when the benefits were paid. This tax treatment could involve an immediate revenue loss, though it would be mitigated if the accounts reduce other tax-preferred saving.

2. Conversely, they could be made taxable when saved and deductible when received. Because the saving generating the individual accounts would still only be taxed once, this tax treatment would have about the same net effect in present-value terms as the deferred tax treatment that is now received by most other defined-contribution pension saving. This tax treatment could involve ultimate federal revenue loss, if the individual accounts reduced other tax-preferred saving.

Notes

Chapter 1

1. The third-rail analogy is taken from the Metro System of Washington, DC, where the power comes from the third rail.

2. The reasoning behind this proposition, explained further below, was first developed by Samuelson (1958).

3. See, for example, Reno and Friedland 1997.

4. The World Bank 1994.

5. Technically, prefunded accounts pay higher rates of return than those implicit in a PAYG system when the economy's real interest rate exceeds its economic growth rate. That in turn happens when the economy-wide saving rate is less than what is known as the Golden Rule saving rate, essentially capital's share of national output. The national saving rate in the United States is clearly less than capital's share, implying that the returns on prefunded accounts should clearly exceed those from a PAYG system.

6. Advisory Council 1997. The Committee for Economic Development 1997 has a very similar proposal.

Chapter 2

1. Social Security and Medicare Boards of Trustees 1997.

2. The polling data are given in Reno and Friedland 1997. The books are Peterson 1996 and Carter and Shipman 1996.

3. Advisory Council 1997.

4. Berkowitz 1997. See also Ball 1988 and Bryce and Friedland 1997.

5. There was brief mention of the DC option in the initial staff report on Social Security, but there seems to have been little such discussion in Congress.

6. While in a legal sense payroll taxes are paid by both employers and employees, if the supply of labor is insensitive to wage changes, as it probably is, it can be shown that the true incidence of the entire payroll tax is on employees. Their pay is lower by approximately the amount their employer contributes. The employer share is then a form of political window-dressing.

7. The precise benefit formula for 1996 is that the PIA equals 90 percent of taxable payrolls up to $5,244, then 32 percent of taxable payrolls from $5,244 to $31,620, then 15 percent of taxable payrolls above $31,620.

8. Normally replacement rates are computed as benefits in the first year of retirement over wages in the last year of work. Here I am substituting average taxable payrolls for the normal denominator.

9. Report of the Advisory Commission to Study the Consumer Price Index 1996.

10. The numbers shown in the table are computed at age 60 for the individual. If prices were stable, the PIA computed at age 60 would then be paid to the individual at age 65. If prices increased between the time the individual was 60 and 65, the PIA would be upgraded in exactly the same proportion. Hence the numbers in table 2.1 can be considered the appropriate real PIA for that individual.

11. There has been an earnings test that reduced Social Security benefits by a third to a half for work done in retirement years up to age 70. In 1996 the Congress eliminated this earnings test for earnings on an amount that rises gradually up to $30,000, though the test is still there for higher earnings. The delayed retirement credit is moving to financial indifference on the basis of pretax income—some economists would prefer the indifference to be based on after-tax income.

12. For more details see National Academy of Social Insurance 1996.

13. Steuerle and Bakija 1994. Just as SSI includes general-revenue assistance for aged individuals regardless of work experience, there is also a SSI Disability Insurance program.

14. Quinn (forthcoming) arrives at similar conclusions on the basis of time series calculations.

15. Burkhauser and Smeeding 1994.

16. See Tobin 1988 and Blinder 1988, for more extensive arguments.

17. Advisory Council 1997.

Chapter 3

1. Social Security and Medicare Boards of Trustees 1997, Advisory Council 1997. The council did criticize the way in which the high- and low-cost options were formed. Now these high- and low-cost scenarios use high- and low-cost assumptions for all key variables simultaneously, an unlikely statistical prospect. Presumably changes in the direction of more statistical realism would reduce the spread between the high- and low-cost outcomes.

2. Advisory Council 1997, appendix.

3. Social Security and Medicare Boards of Trustees 1997.

4. The total fertility rate for any year is the average number of children who would be born to a woman in her lifetime, if she were to experience the birth rates by age, observed or assumed, of the selected year, and if she were to survive the entire child-bearing period.

5. It is sometimes argued that this way of looking at things overstates the burdens of an aging society because there will at the same time be declining numbers of young dependents. While true, this argument means surprisingly little for the federal budget because spending on the aged is far higher than spending on the young. Most spending on the young is for public schooling, generally paid for by state and local governments, but even then much less per capita than spending on the aged.

6. The calculation is given by Auerbach 1997.

7. This is a simplified description of a proposition first proved by Samuelson (1958).

8. Panis and Lillard 1996 show that when the greater life expectancy of high-wage individuals is factored in, the apparent redistribution in Social Security is cut substantially.

9. The *present value* is a financial concept used to convert future tax payments and benefits into common terms, as if these benefits were to be received at the present. All future payments are "discounted" by the

interest rate on government bonds, as if government bonds were the standard of comparison.

As was asserted earlier, when labor supply is reasonably inelastic, even the payroll tax actually paid by the employer is probably shifted over onto the employee. Hence it makes sense to consider both contributions on the payment side—a typical employee is paying her own payroll tax directly and the employer's contribution on her wage indirectly.

10. The figure shows a puzzling drop in money's worth ratios for workers born in the 1950s. The explanation is that these workers spent much of their careers working and paying taxes when real interest rates were abnormally high. In this sense they could have gotten good returns from funds invested in bonds, and the Social Security return, evaluated in comparison to the bond rate, suffers by comparison.

Chapter 4

1. The technical panel in Advisory Council 1997, Quinn forthcoming, and Steuerle and Bakija 1994 all have lists of goals of Social Security reform that look somewhat different from mine. Both have one goal that refers to equity across generations (or individual equity), which more or less is covered by my rate-of-return goal. Quinn and the technical panel have another goal referring to national saving (or economic growth), which is close to what I label long-term economic affordability. The technical panel and Steuerle and Bakija also have goals that refer to minimizing economic distortions, my near-term economic affordability. I lump all the other goals in both lists under the category of preserving the social protections of Social Security.

2. See Feldstein and Samwick 1997, Kotlikoff 1997, and Devine 1997 for further discussion.

3. Many of these retirement age provisions are analyzed by Mitchell 1991.

4. The first person to put national saving on the agenda as an important problem with Social Security was Feldstein (1974). He is still a strong supporter of higher national saving, or of devices for more prefunding (see Feldstein and Samwick 1997). The Council of Economic Advisers (1997) treats national saving in the context of the maturation of the Social Security program. A recent paper discussing the saving issue in an international context is Bosworth and Burtless 1997.

Chapter 5

1. Advisory Council 1997.
2. Steuerle and Bakija 1994.
3. Advisory Commission to Study the Consumer Price Index 1996.
4. An illustrative plan is given by Phillips 1996.
5. Many of these criticisms are made by Burtless 1996.
6. Such a plan is proposed by Bosworth 1996.
7. To compute actuarial balance and rates of return when some retirement funds were invested in common stocks, it was necessary to make assumptions about the likely future performance of stocks. Dickson (1997) studied the matter thoroughly and found that historically stocks have outperformed bonds by 4.3 percent per year, the difference that was incorporated in these forecasts. The advisory council report gives sensitivity calculations, in case this premium is less than 4.3 percent.
8. Advisory Council 1997.
9. For a favorable comment on central fund equity investment, see Diamond 1996a.
10. Advisory Council 1997. See also Feldstein and Samwick 1997 and Kotlikoff 1997 for similar approaches.
11. Diamond 1993 elaborates on these issues.
12. Goodfellow and Schieber (1997) consider variances and show that in most cases the PSA plan still performs reasonably well on rate-of-return grounds.
13. Advisory Council 1997. The Kerrey-Simpson plan of the 104th Congress is described and costed out in the advisory council report. The Committee for Economic Development (1997) has offered a very similar plan. Thompson, in Salisbury 1997, gives a defense of this general approach. The approach is also quite popular in the polls—see Yakoboski 1997 for some general polling results.
14. Those workers who already have private-pension saving on top of Social Security and who are sufficiently rational to compute these things finely may reduce their own pension saving in response to mandatory DC accounts. But since many workers do not save on top of Social Security, and many others may be creatures of habit, this large group of workers is likely to increase their saving. Overall national saving would then necessarily rise.
15. An example of where public management of DC accounts works well is the Federal Employees Thrift Plan. As with the IA accounts, federal

thrift plan accounts are individually owned, not in the federal budget. Employees choose among constrained portfolios of stocks and bonds, exactly as they would in the IA plan.

Chapter 6

1. World Bank 1994.

2. Aged dependency rates of 50 percent, which imply that there are two workers for every aged individual, seem about the same as those shown for the United States in figure 3.3. In fact the dependency rates shown in table 6.1 are higher because the denominator is all individuals aged 15–64, not just active workers.

3. This liability of $2.5 trillion corresponds to the payroll gap of 2.2 percent. I use this figure for comparability with the others shown.

4. Disney and Johnson 1997.

5. Persson 1997. Individual accounts invested in bonds will earn the going real interest rate, and those in stocks could earn even more, if past trends in rates of return continue. Both rates of return are above those of a PAYG system for countries that save less than the share of capital in national output, as most countries now do.

6. Edey 1997.

7. Barreto and Mitchell forthcoming, Edwards 1997.

8. Barreto and Mitchell forthcoming, Edwards 1997, and Diamond 1996b.

9. Barreto and Mitchell forthcoming.

Appendix

From Advisory Council 1997.

1. If a worker dies before reaching retirement age, the accumulated funds would be held for the surviving spouse and would be available (in the form of an annuity) when the surviving spouse became eligible for widow(er)'s benefits at age 60. If the worker did not leave a surviving spouse, the funds would go to the worker's estate.

2. Benefits would continue to be available on an actuarially reduced basis for workers and spouses at age 62, and for aged spouses at age 60.

References

Advisory Commission to Study the Consumer Price Index. 1996. *Toward a More Accurate Measure of the Cost of Living*. Washington, DC: Government Printing Office.

Advisory Council on Social Security. 1997. *Report of the 1994–96 Advisory Council on Social Security*. Vols. 1–2. Washington, DC: Government Printing Office.

Auerbach, Alan J. 1997. "Quantifying the Current US Fiscal Imbalance." National Tax Association Symposium.

Ball, Robert M. 1988. "Social Security across the Generations." In *Social Security and Economic Well-Being across Generations,* ed. John R. Gist. Washington, DC: American Association of Retired Persons.

Barreto, Flavio Ataliba, and Olivia S. Mitchell. Forthcoming. "Privatizing Latin American Retirement Systems." Paper presented at St. Louis Federal Reserve Bank conference on Social Security, April 1997. To be published in *Review.*

Berkowitz, Edward D. 1997. "The Historical Development of Social Security in the United States." In *Social Security in the 21st Century,* ed. Eric R. Kingson and James H. Schulz. New York: Oxford University Press.

Bipartisan Commission on Entitlements and Tax Reform. 1994. *Interim Report to the President*. Washington, DC: Government Printing Office.

Blinder, Alan S. 1988. "Why Is the Government in the Pension Business?" In *Social Security and Private Pensions,* ed. Susan M. Wachter. Lexington, MA: DC Heath and Company.

Bosworth, Barry P. 1996. "Fund Accumulation: How Much? How Managed?" In *Social Security: What Role for the Future?* ed. Peter A. Diamond,

David C. Lindeman, and Howard Young. Washington, DC: National Academy of Social Insurance.

Bosworth, Barry P., and Gary Burtless. 1997. "Social Security Reform in a Global Context." Paper presented at Boston Federal Reserve Bank conference on Social Security, conference series no. 41, June 1997. In *Social Security Reform: Links to Saving, Investment, and Growth,* ed. Steven A. Sass and Robert K. Triest. Boston: Federal Reserve Bank of Boston.

Bryce, David V., and Robert B. Friedland. 1997. "Economic Security: An Overview of Social Security." In *Assessing Social Security Reform Alternatives,* ed. Dallas L. Salisbury. Washington, DC: Employee Benefit Research Institute.

Bureau of the Census. 1993. *Poverty in the United States: 1992.* Current Population Reports, Series P60–185. Washington, DC: Government Printing Office.

Burkhauser, Richard V., and Timothy M. Smeeding. 1994. "Social Security Reform: A Budget Neutral Approach to Reducing Older Women's Disproportionate Risk of Poverty." Maxwell School of Citizenship and Public Affairs Policy Brief, Syracuse University, no. 2.

Burtless, Gary. 1996. "Social Security Income and Taxation: Four Views on the Role of Means Testing." In *Social Security: What Role for the Future?* ed. Peter A. Diamond, David C. Lindeman, and Howard Young. Washington, DC: National Academy of Social Insurance.

Carter, Marshall N., and William G. Shipman. 1996. *Promises to Keep: Saving Social Security's Dream.* Washington, DC: Regnery Publishing.

Committee for Economic Development. 1997. *Fixing Social Security.* New York: Committee for Economic Development.

Council of Economic Advisers. 1997. *Economic Report of the President.* Washington, DC: Government Printing Office.

Davis, E. Phillip. 1997. "Public Pensions, Pension Reform, and Fiscal Policy." European Monetary Institute, staff paper no. 5, March 1997. Mimeo.

Devine, Theresa J. 1997. "Demographics, Social Security Reform, and Labor Supply." Paper presented at Boston Federal Reserve Bank conference on Social Security, conference series no. 41, June 1997. In *Social Security Reform: Links to Saving, Investment, and Growth,* ed. Steven A. Sass and Robert K. Triest. Boston: Federal Reserve Bank of Boston.

Diamond, Peter A. 1993. "Issues in Social Insurance." Nancy L. Schwartz

Lecture, J. L. Kellogg School of Management, Northwestern University.

———. 1996a. "Proposals to Restructure Social Security." *Journal of Economic Perspectives* 10 (summer): 67–88.

———. 1996b. "Social Security Reform in Chile: An Economist's Perspective." In *Social Security: What Role for the Future?* ed. Peter A. Diamond, David C. Lindeman, and Howard Young. Washington, DC: National Academy of Social Insurance.

Dickson, Joel. 1997. "Analysis of Financial Conditions Surrounding Individual Accounts." In *Report of the 1994–96 Advisory Council on Social Security,* vol. 2. Washington, DC: Government Printing Office.

Disney, Richard, and Paul Johnson. 1997. "The United Kingdom: A Working System of Pensions." Paper presented at Kiel conference on Social Security, June 1997. Mimeo.

Edey, Malcolm. 1997. "Retirement Income Policy in Australia." Paper presented at Boston Federal Reserve Bank conference on Social Security, conference series no. 41, June 1997. In *Social Security Reform: Links to Saving, Investment, and Growth,* ed. Steven A. Sass and Robert K. Triest. Boston: Federal Reserve Bank of Boston.

Edwards, Sebastian. 1997. "Chile: Radical Change towards a Funded Pension System." Paper presented at Kiel conference on Social Security, June 1997. Mimeo.

Feldstein, Martin S. 1974. "Social Security, Induced Retirement, and Aggregate Capital Accumulation." *Journal of Political Economy* 82 (September–October): 905–26.

Feldstein, Martin S., and Andrew Samwick. 1997. "The Transition Path in Privatizing Social Security." Paper presented at Kiel conference on Social Security, June 1997. Mimeo.

Goodfellow, Gordon P., and Sylvester J. Schieber. 1997. *Social Security Reform: Implications of Individual Accounts on the Distribution of Benefits.* Washington, DC: Watson Wyatt Worldwide.

Grad, Susan. 1997. *Income of the Aged: 1994.* Washington, DC: Social Security Administration.

Hochstein, Madelyn. 1995. *A Study of Public Values and Attitudes.* Washington, DC: American Association of Retired Persons.

Kotlikoff, Laurence J. 1997. "Privatizing Social Security in the United States: Why and How." In *Fiscal Policy: Lessons from Economic Research,* ed. Alan J. Auerbach. Cambridge: MIT Press.

Mitchell, Olivia S. 1991. "Social Security Reforms and Poverty among Older Dual-Earner Couples." *Population Economics* 4, no. 4 (spring): 281–93.

National Academy of Social Insurance. 1996. *Advisory Council on Social Security Plans.* National Academy of Social Insurance.

Panis, Constantijn W. A., and Lee A. Lillard. 1996. "Socioeconomic Differentials in the Returns to Social Security." Rand Corporation working paper.

Persson, Mats. 1997. "Sweden: Cutting the Welfare State Back to Size." Paper presented at Kiel conference on Social Security, June 1997. Mimeo.

Peterson, Peter G. 1996. "Will America Grow Up before It Grows Old?" *Atlantic Monthly,* May, 55–86.

Phillips, Martha. 1996. "Social Security Income and Taxation: Four Views on the Role of Means Testing." In *Social Security: What Role for the Future?* ed. Peter A. Diamond, David C. Lindeman, and Howard Young. Washington, DC: National Academy of Social Insurance.

Quinn, Joseph F. "Criteria for Social Security Reform." In *Prospects for Social Security Reform,* ed. Olivia Mitchell, Robert Myers, and Howard Young. Philadelphia: University of Pennsylvania Press, forthcoming.

Reno, Virginia P., and Robert B. Friedland. 1997. "Strong Support but Low Confidence: What Explains the Contradiction?" In *Social Security in the 21st Century,* ed. Eric R. Kingson and James H. Schulz. New York: Oxford University Press.

Samuelson, Paul A. 1958. "An Exact Consumption-Loan Model of Interest with or without the Social Contrivance of Money." *Journal of Political Economy* (December): 219–34.

Social Security and Medicare Boards of Trustees. 1997. *Status of the Social Security and Medicare Programs.* Washington, DC: Government Printing Office.

Steuerle, C. Eugene, and Jon M. Bakija. 1994. *Retooling Social Security for the 21st Century.* Washington, DC: Urban Institute.

Thompson, Lawrence H. 1997. "The Case for the Individual Accounts Option." In *Assessing Social Security Reform Alternatives,* ed. Dallas L. Salisbury. Washington, DC: Employee Benefit Research Institute.

Tobin, James. 1988. "The Future of Social Security: One Economist's Assessment." In *Social Security: Beyond the Rhetoric of Crisis,* ed. Theodore R. Marmor and Jerry L. Mashaw. Princeton: Princeton University Press.

REFERENCES

World Bank. 1994. *Averting the Old Age Crisis.* New York: Oxford University Press.

Yakoboski, Paul. 1997. "Daring to Touch the Third Rail." In *Assessing Social Security Reform Alternatives,* ed. Dallas L. Salisbury. Washington, DC: Employee Benefit Research Institute.

Index